Winning is not Always Success

Small effort for big impact

Attention Authors

'We Convert Fighters into Writers'. That's the motto of Manas Publications since more than four decades. Our message to the world is that India can win the battle not only by the bullet but also by the pen. There is no dearth of intellectuals in our country, but their knowledge is confined to them only. No sincere effort has been made by any other publisher to channelise their knowledge in national interest. That is why the talent of a large number of intellectuals remains latent. An author transforms his knowledge into a manuscript, and it is our job to spread his/her knowledge by converting it into a beautiful book. For over four decades, Manas has been motivating the intellectuals by publishing their manuscripts and would like to publish your manuscript too. If you or your colleagues have any manuscript ready for publication or are working on it, kindly contact us with detailed synopsis and list of contents. We will transform your work into a valuable publication. If you wish, we can also suggest you the suitable subjects for writing the books related to your area of expertise. Manas is known for its publishing quality and commitments. We take utmost care in production and give wide publicity to the book as well as its author through our national and international distribution network.

Winning is not Always Success

Small effort for big impact

Abhinav, PMP

Manas Publications
(We Convert Fighters into Writers)
New Delhi-110002 (INDIA)

MANAS PUBLICATIONS
(Publishers for IAS, IPS, IFS, IRS, Defence, Press, Judges etc.)
(Publishers, Distributors, Importers & Exporters)
4402/5-A, Ansari Road (Opp. HDFC Bank)
Darya Ganj, New Delhi-110 002 (India)
Off: ✆ 011-23260783, 23265523, Res: 011-23842660
Fax: 011-23272766
E-mail: manaspublications@gmail.com
manaspublications@yahoo.com
Website: www.manaspublications.in

ISBN: 978-81-7049-501-7
₹ 495/-

Designed at
Manas Publications

Printed in India at
Printways, Delhi
and published by Mrs Suman Lata for
Manas Publications,
4402/5-A, Ansari Road, (Opp HDFC Bank),
Darya Ganj, New Delhi-110 002 (INDIA)

"Winners do not take it all,
Losers also have every reason to smile
to strike big"

"Let's create magic for success, for
ourselves and for the country"
So, don't think, just read it

Preface

How to die in peace knowing that you are successful

This book has been written keeping in mind the Indian middle class who are the real contributors to the country's growth and who have a zeal and talent to achieve greater heights in their life. This book is not just about winning, you have to be a good human being to sustain your success.

Many people in this world have achieved monetary success, still they lack the aura of being called a good human being and are successful in their life because of their selfish and arrogant behaviour. As the country, organization, or an individual climbs the ladder of success, they leave the basic or fundamental parameters of success (care and passion) in their recycle bins and ride on a complacency syndrome, (We are the best and We can do no wrong) try extreme and sometimes unusual measures to please their masters, convert their natural success into artificial ones. If you keep things simple (Hard to done), minimize your work fronts and get people along your success path and remember God, success will come to you, you need not have to run after success.

Today, India is going through a phase of a famous Urdu saying ***"Har sakh pe ullu baitha hai anjamey gulisthan kya hoga"***. This means everywhere there is confusion and indecisions galore and God only knows what will happen. The book will illustrate real life examples and experiences to find out the nuances of life to become a real successful person and India should win rather individuals. The idea here is not to criticize or praise anybody but to drive the point of view only. This book is a reality check for all of us, as India has been put on the backburner and left sulking.

The idea floated in the book is not to achieve a super human life but a life full of satisfaction and happiness. We have a great fascination for complexities but we never adopt simplicity to deal with life. It is a must read book for the Indian middle class and people in general. You will find several books written with too many jargons which cannot be followed. This book will help you in giving directions with simple logic and what are the minimum efforts required to maximize your success and will have the desired information at single place in simple understandable language. The book will again take you to the drawing board to reinvent and rejuvenate yourself.

This book is written with *Dil Se* (From the heart) without any pre-conceived notions, prejudices and biases, and any relation with the thoughts or ideas presented in the book and with other thinkers or books are merely co-incidental. Some of the ideas given in the book may sound familiar but the same ideas we never follow in life. Lessons learnt are for others, but I am perfect, is what people believe today. This book is for us and should be read in entirety to get the real crux out of it, instead of reading a few chapters.

The idea of writing the book is not to get literary accolades and present lengthy philosophy (not on More the Merrier Concept) but to highlight the essence of the theme to stimulate people for positive thinking and rationalizing their perceptions. The readers will enjoy reading the book which will help in generating new or contradictory ideas.

Acknowledgement

The author acknowledges the common man of India and also the diverse culture of India which has inspired him for writing this book. Special acknowledgments go to all those Known and Unknown faces who have given my thought process a real kick. Last but not the least, I thank all the well-wishers including my Maa (Mother) who has been my biggest strength.

Contents

Part-1

Professional Winning

Mainly related to make the professional winning always a success and environment required to succeed with some project management concepts and approach (only takeaways mentioned in the book, for details refer the Google baba) coupled with some real life backing.

Introduction

"Who is a successful person?"

Life is like a linear programming equation, you have to maximise your potential and minimise your failures under various constraints to deal with the reality of life. In this competitive world, life is like a high pressurised pipe having a lot of holes, plugging one hole increases the pressure on the other holes and you have to work hard to prevent it from leakages. It is an era of multitasking for survival. We are today working on a weighted average basis. Variability or complexities of life has denied us to pursue our passion. The best thing you can do to have one sigma deviation from the mean life to say with 95% confidence or consistency or performance level that you are doing okay. Only God has zero defect performance level. Success and failures require multiple differentiation and integration to get the desired results and maxima and minima of your life. Do not clap your success before it is actually clapped. Life is like a project which has a start and end date and it is a unique endeavour by all of us to create a unique product for the mankind. Like project, life also has competing constraints of scope, cost, time and doing a balancing act to have a good quality life, is possible only by employing risk mitigating strategies every now and then. This can be achieved by way of focused (**incremental**) approach and mostly taking decisions based on facts and figures, to have more probability of success. Today, most unlikely is likely.

Humans can never become God, only God is Supreme. Those who are willing and try to analyze their weaknesses and failures will become successful in life and can sustain it on a long term basis. However, majority of humans like to remain in the state of inertia. They need a jump start as it happens when your car battery is not functioning properly.

Success should not be measured in terms of winning; it should be measured in terms of winning hearts. How you are being perceived by the society, your family and your peers, seniors and juniors at work place is most important for a successful life. Be a catalyst for changing the skyline of your surroundings and paradigm shift in the mind set of people.

We are all aware of the recent recession which was brought by the sub-prime lending, leading to the collapse of the major financial institutions in USA , bankruptcy of General Motors where they focused only on their brand image (We are the Best) rather than improving the system inefficiencies as done by Toyota by leveraging their outsourcing benefits of quality and price to customers, fall of Russia from superpower status was due to their absurd policy that they can survive by turning blind eye to the events happening in the rest of the world and fall of Tiger Woods from greatness to not so great are some of the recent examples of a fall out of the complacency syndrome.

One can find various books written on how to have a habit of winning, how to achieve success and how to win in life. But the matter of fact is that one should not AIM at winning always but how to remain level headed, polite and dignified in their work and behaviour despite so many pulls and pressures. You will find so called successful people more often lose their temper on the slight provocation and their behavioral aspect needs a lot to be desired. Life is too short to have these negative shades in our life.

Are these people successful? The answer is a big NO. The simple reason is that they are setting a bad example for the society although people idolize them. People will always test your patience. There are two kinds of people who normally are not able to digest success and get carried away. One with little or poor academic background and one who believes they have all the wisdom in the world and have one stop solutions for every problem the world is facing today. The former can be easily moulded by money mongers as they do not have the visualization of being used, while the latter fall out happens due to larger than life image which breeds arrogance.

The other major important issue here is "Success at what cost?"

In the pursuit of excellence, super success, name and fame we are forgetting, simple old wisdom "Health is Wealth". The live example for such ignorance is Michael Jackson, one of the most famous singers of our times who lost the battle of life prematurely because he made himself the slave of drugs to cope with the pulls and pressure of success. Such people are self-obsessed and fear of rejection in them is paramount. Please remember, you will never enjoy success unless your health is okay. You can have drugs and medicine to ward-off the competition, but ultimately you will be undone by yourself. The self-killing of Michael Jackson was in bad taste while the slow death of Steve Jobs, the Apple founder made him a successful martyr of life. Today life is so hectic even breathing requires some space for breathing. Although our life span has increased, 40 has become new 60 where body immune system is more prone to the attack of diseases as body organs malfunctions more often due to continuous fatigue and forces people to mentally retire at 40 than at 60.

So, friends many persons even if they have not achieved super success like many famous personalities, are really successful in their life as they have remained calm during adversity and plan meticulously to deal with uncertainties. They have not only brought happiness to their life but also spread happiness around.

For a person to be successful in life, he should be educated, honest to himself, and have integrity of highest order, ability to analyze things before jumping to conclusions and take care of stakeholders in his life.

For the country to be successful, foster culture of team work and avoid individual worship.

The next few chapters will give you the necessary inputs with real life examples and experiences to make your life successful and your surroundings a better place.

What is required is Planning?

You are planning to fail or failing to get any plan in place.

Planning your life is the key to start a journey for a successful life. The question one should ask is what he or she wants to achieve in life. The majority of middle class want to live the life of a film star or want to have quick money without putting in real effort.

The backbone of the middle class is their intellectual power which is the driving force of the country's GDP. The middle class who have limited earning and resources cannot have the luxury to take risks in life. Money is the major constraint for them to break-free. Constantly looking for an opportunity and upgrading yourself is the way to achieve greater heights. It is like a refresh button on computer screen. Knowledge power is what is to be seen as success mantra. "Learn More and Earn More" but never go after earning with illegal ways. The objectives and goals have to be clearly defined in terms of being achievable. There is no short cut to success; "patience" is the key.

Rafael Nadal, Dykowich, Leander Paes, Ivan Lendal and some of the few players including others whose name are not mentioned here, have made their mark simply by sheer hard work and dedication. They look for incremental approach in life.They are finishers and DO not easily let things go beyond their control till they put the final nail in the coffin as compared to Tendulkars of this world who have greater talent but are NOT finishers always.

When you look at people like Rafel Nadal and Dykowich, you find they have never given up their attitude and they have come out with something extraordinary when the chips are down. They fight each point as if their life depend on it.

When you see a 100 meters race, till 90 meters everybody is at par, it is the last moment burst which decides the winner (especially when you see Usain Bolt doing the same thing time and again).

The idea here is to make a distinction on how you go about your task—Meticulous planning or simply rushing. Success in any field of life is all about doing what you believe in. Most of the failure happens at the last hurdle.

There are people in this world who do everything right till the last moment, but fail to clear the finish line when the moment of truth comes. Never celebrate before success is actually achieved. It is like downloading something on a mobile, suddenly after 99% download, message comes download unsuccessful.

Here are a few tips to go about the job being done:

- Objectives and goals have to be defined in clear terms and plan has to be made accordingly. Planning by way of work-break down structure and then sequencing the activities to find out the critical path (Longest path in the network) where you do not have any buffer time. Any slackness on this path will derail your planning. Backbone of planning are the lessons learnt and keeping them in your kitty is treasures.

- Keep things simple and straight. Never plan for super human success.
- Keep things in your control and refresh when certain milestones are achieved.
- Do not let negativity creep into your mind and focus on your job.
- Do cost-benefit analysis and risk assessment of your actions every now and then, which will let you know where you are. Have a fall back plan in place by doing a decision tree analysis where you have the probability of success for various scenarios.
- Regroup after each failure and do a quick SWOT analysis.
- Always have words "Thank You and Sorry" in your dictionary. Use them in abundance whenever required. However, be assertive, do not let others take you lightly.
- Try to learn from your juniors also and walk with them and be ready to accept the mistakes or criticisms.
- Follow `We' before `I'.
- Try to be skewed towards saying "Yes" than "No" to overcome initial fissures with boss or juniors.
- Compete with yourself for continuous improvement.
- Command respect not demand respect.
- Do not dress up shabbily. Manage dress code to have an impact statement.

- Try to keep yourself appraised with the surroundings and learn from the real life experiences.
- Differentiate yourself by having new skill sets under your belly and build upon your success.
- Sometimes use your self-leisure time for new ideas for your life. Listening to good music is the greatest stress buster.
- Remember God for every success and other stakeholders who are your well-wishers and keep failures for yourselves.
- Do your bit in social gatherings like crack a joke, sing a song, rock the floor kind of stuff to reinvent yourself.
- Keep your family happy for your success both at professional and personal front.
- Most important of all, keep track of your health. Be an early riser and walk some distance for your health and fresh ideas. Most important is to have at least 4-5 hours of sound sleep under your belly to have your metabolism and brain working.

Here, I will explain the importance of having a dress code in place as it is the only thing people often forget and this is most important aspect to give you first mover advantage at any place in your life

- ➢ Dress for success
- ➢ Reflects the culture of the organization besides your personality.
- ➢ "First Impression is not the last but lasting impression"

and

The first impression is made by your appearance.

- A flawless appearance can bring inner peace and sense of security.
- It gives a whole professional dimension to the individual and organization at large that "We Mean Business."
- Proper dress code commands respect from customers, stakeholders and gives an " Aura" to the entire organization.

In a nutshell, a dress code gives you business oriented presentable look which emanates from wearing a neat formal dress, having a fresh and bright face, having a dignified hairstyle , wearing well maintained shoes; all to give you an upright and bold character.

Most of the successful persons are self-driven and restless. They use their common sense and logical steps in achieving their targets. Today common sense is very uncommon. Common sense only comes when you have clarity of thoughts. There are always wrong ways of doing right things. Successful people always look for right way of doing right things (Optimizing the methods of doing under constraints of resources) and they do not do anything differently as some book suggests. Today question papers of IIT and IIM are the toughest in India to crack. This requires lot of practice and hard work and common sense. There is a fine line between success and failure in such examinations. Question papers normally range from simple/ moderate (More in numbers- carries less marks) to toughest (Less in numbers - carries maximum marks). You need to figure out the simpler and moderate questions. Try to solve only these questions within the time limit to get volume based success rather going in for tougher questions. These questions require coherence of concepts (common sense) in a logical manner. The reason we do not regularly use our common sense is that we have laid back attitude and wait for others to do it for ourselves rather than analyzing or using our critical thinking. The idea here is to explain that you need to assess the situations before shooting the messenger. Do 20:80 analysis of each activity as 20% is responsible for failure and focus on those areas. Start using your brain otherwise somebody else will take the position you deserve.

One time effort will help you to enjoy economies of scale. The sustainability of success is your ability. Never celebrate before you actually strike the winning ball otherwise it will take you away from the winning post. One moment of madness as happened in the life of many successful persons will take away the sheen of your glory.

Conflict and Ego Management

"Success with minimum heart burns is a joy forever."

If you are okay and some body is not okay, then conflict starts. Conflict is the biggest hurdle in getting the things move in life. As a high school student, where you have to maximize your potential, most of them in today's technological advancing worlds get into conflict easily with parents, teachers and the world in general. The energy has to be channelized towards the goals as these years are building blocks for future achievements. Friends are important but career is what one should look for achieving greater heights. Do not try to overdo and act as per your potential. Get professional degree to get a foot hold for your dreams and survival in this mad world. Try to differentiate yourself and get yourself in the competition. Conflicts should be taken in positives only although it has negative connotation. We find in one advertisement of Surf Excel detergent (Hindi): "Dagg Achey Hotey Hain" –means Stains are Good. Conflicts are the breeding ground for better and logical decisions.

When your have problem confronting attitude, dealing with conflicts will help you to increase effectiveness, better co-ordination among various groups, foster more positive vibes in the entire organization, better risk and change management, and possible positive outcomes are vital for the timely resolution of problems within the timelines. People will always judge you by your achievements in first go and then by your behaviour. Try to win hearts and be a good human being to succeed in life. Talk to yourself regularly in the mirror and try to collaborate, compete, compromise to resolve conflicts in life and make use of the conflicts in improving yourself rather than blaming others for the mishaps. Try to treat your conflicts as friends, as they are your true success builders. Good humour will make you feel relaxed when the moment of truth comes.

Ego is the biggest killer of success. Ego in simple terms is I before We. Positive Ego breeds self-respect and accommodating other view-points, while Negative Ego breeds larger than life image downsizing others, arrogance, complacency and ignorance as well. Hurt Egos are the major source of wars and conflicts all around the world. In meetings, you often find people get firing from the management for slip-ups and some time for no specific reasons. This is mainly because people want to stamp their authority without analyzing the situation. Bad behaviour and bad decision will ruin your success. Keep your ego aside and see life from the perspective of others. Be good to your well-wishers and also try to be generous towards your competitors. Look upon others as sources of inspiration and contribute for the future of the human race. Remember success with minimum heart burns is a joy forever.

Johari window will give the egoist person some enlightment

The Johari Window is a technique created by Joseph Luft and Harrington Ingham in 1955 in the United States. It is used to help people better understand their relationship with self and others. It is used primarily in self-help groups and corporate settings as a heuristic exercise.

Johari window

	Known to self	Not known to self
Known to others	Arena	Blind Spot
Not Known to Others	Façade	Unknown

Open or Arena

This quadrant represents traits of the subjects that both they and their peers are aware of. Make yourself refreshed by removing the negative or grey areas.

Hidden or Façade

This quadrant represents traits of the subjects that only subject is aware of not their peers. Here comes your weakest or strongest area where you are better informed and only you can improve for greater heights.

Blind Spot

This quadrant represents traits of the subjects that only peers are aware of, not the subject. Try to get your blind spots in your armory (Feedback). This is what a egoist person does not want and keeps others at bay.

Unknown

This quadrant represents unknown traits not known to both subject and peers. Our potential is unknown to us, and others. The takeaway is that we have to re-invent ourselves and talk to ourselves in the mirror and make ourselves counted.

There is one famous doha (Lines) by the famous poet of ancient India, Kabir for the egoist person

Bura Jo Dekhen Mein Chala, Bura Na Milya Koi,
Jo dil khoja apnoo mujse bura na koi.

It means, if we dig deep in ourselves, we will find lot

of shortcomings and we should try to remove that before finding the same in others.

Leadership Skills

"We Mean Business."

Not everyone in this world is a born leader. However, leadership skills are very important to sustain success.

Some of the desired skill sets are as follows:

- Act as a champion and a catalyst.
- Able to resolve conflicts.
- Able to anticipate and visualize problems or risks, confront them - provide alternatives and contingency plan.
- Able to switch from being a specialist to being a generalist.
- Able to facilitate, delegate and most importantly accommodate
- Should have strategic and analytical thinking skills - constantly looking for an opportunity to improve upon the benchmarks.

- Most importantly, should have human touch and ego moderated.

To be successful at your work place, try to do the following simple things:

- Try to listen to the problems of your subordinates (both personnel and work-front) to get the best out of them.
- Try to have parity in dealing with your subordinates as far as possible, by being their mentor.
- Try to counsel and motivate and foster culture of team work.
- Try to explain and appraise management of the great work and challenges faced by the team.
- Try to make stress-free culture.
- Make problem–confronting and out of box thinking teams.
- The most difficult part is appraisals in the organization. Pick and Choose policy in appraisals based on whims and fancies instead of focusing on the candidate potential, sincerity and their willingness to take extra responsibility, may end up in picking a candidate who will not have the desired conviction for taking decisions. You have to be like Jumman the character in the Hindi story "Panch Parmeshwar" written by Munshi Premchand, in which the moral of the story is that the person sitting on the highest pedestal should be free and fair in his judgment without any bias. So, being the leader you have to recognize and reward on rationale basis.

People who plan, manage conflict, and have desirable leadership skills can sustain and manage success. Dhoni and Ganguly, the captain of Indian Team with their limited capability and good leadership have managed to get the Indian Team going. They have shown the importance of team work which the Australian team had demonstrated over the years. Leaders who take decisions on their whims and fancies without consulting team or analyzing the situations are bound to be a failure. There are people like late Russi Mody (Ex CEO of TATA) who effectively managed the show at TATA due to his good human touch approach.

To find out a natural leader, just place a small boulder in the middle of the road, you will find majority of us will pass the road blaming the system, but the real leader will get the obstacle removed and make the system work on a continuous basis and get the people involved. The idea here is to just explain that leaders command respect by their action and they do it by themselves for the benefit of others.

In India, majority of political leaders and corporate leaders, barring a few leaders, have not contributed much for improving the human development index of this country or increasing the people purchasing power. Corporate leaders are quite busy in maximizing their wealth, while some do little bit of corporate social responsibility but they are not forthcoming to make this great country self-reliant. We have become increasingly a debating society, providing lip service, individual worship culture rather than improving the systems and implementing the laws already existing instead we want more laws to be made. We Indians are great planners but fail to execute. The reason we do not work collectively is that we have our ego clashes. The cause already lost, the objectives already lost, what remain are hurt egos. The Anna Movement is the fall out of such egos.

Indian leadership elected by the people has great

responsibility to make this happen. Corruption and lack of accountability is what is hurting India and progress of the country. People like E. Sreedharan-Metro Man who are the real Bharat Ratna should be idolized and their motto of "We Mean Business" should be incorporated in the working culture.

In the recent Commonwealth Games besieged with controversies, held in 2010 in Delhi, people of Delhi had shown great discipline during traffic movements and policing was excellent which otherwise always finds napping. If systems are in place, alive and kicking, India can at least give China a run for their money. The success of Commonwealth Games from inauguration to closing has demonstrated that with people support and leadership involved, India can deliver the final knockout punch.

India is heading towards a failed democracy as high percentage of people are still below poverty line and fruits of democracy have not reached them. Earlier, kings used to take stock of their people, human development index, in the nights or through their *guptchars* (Government Informers) and take criticisms in a positive manner to improve the systems of delivery. The same concern is somewhat lost today.

The idea here is to have implementation of systems, fostering a culture of discipline which will definitely improve the lives of the poor people and economy at large. For anybody to succeed in this world, he should have the right kind of environment like in China, where self-driven people are the strength or the driving force of their economy.

What is important is even if you are not head of any organization, in whatever capacity you are presently in, can make a difference to your family, society and country at large having the above qualities. You can become real winner by helping others, making friendly surroundings and making the future generation also a winner. If you have contributed a little bit in your life without hurting mostly and delivered in a constructive fashion, then you will have a peaceful death. Do not plan too much, start fresh from your home, give your children real morale booster thoughts, empower your stakeholders in life with positive thinking, you are a winner.

Today what is required is to reinvent ourselves, plan and work for success, be a change manager for the society keeping aside ego and selfish desires in whatever capacity you are in. Do not belittle your effort, you are equally important.

Positivity Skills

"Behavioural aspect + Listening Skills + Communication Skills + Positive Attitude define Positivity."

This is one of the most important things to have success on a sustainable basis. This is somewhat related to positive attitude which many books on success have talked about. However, being positive is good, but not so good when things get worse. The term used here takes care of things when you are in an adverse situation. Life is like a learning curve where you are judged by others.

A man's success should be judged by his actions and behavioural aspect. Most of the time a successful person gets irritated with the slight provocation and criticism which shows his real character.

People will always look upon you in negative shade and try to pull you down. What is required is to take positivity out of those criticisms and try to make your weakness as your strength. Try to win your competitors with your good behaviour and gesture. Try to read between the lines and turn criticism and failure into success.

Right from your school days and in real life scenario, everything will not get as per your wish. Try to accept reality, your potential and plan accordingly. Work hard for your success, improve your interaction with others, be polite and have faith in God and yourself.

Listening skills are equally important especially in a work-place scenario as it will help in improvement in relationship among peers, subordinates and seniors. Most of the times, we want to put across our viewpoint, without giving patient hearing to others to get their view-point examined. Listening requires great deal of maturity and patience. Shouting at the top of your voice will not make you a likable person. Success is when you listen and resolve the issue, rather creating heart burns. Kiran Bedis, Arvind Kejriwals of this world might have got initial winning strike rate, but because of their sheer arrogance and not listening to other viewpoints, resulted in their failure. Listening will not only give you solution to a problem in a more democratic manner but also improve your chances of increasing your admirers. **Listening is reverse knowledge transfer.**

You will find at your work place or at home or in the

society, a person who listens to others, problems in a patient manner gets the best rewards in terms of making things moving in the right direction. And people will respect his wisdom.

Listening helps in analyzing the things in the right perspective and improving success rate on sustainable basis.

Communication goes hand in hand with listening skills, the clarity of thought and uncluttered mind delivers right communication. How you communicate is what you are. It is always said when you have got your home-work done, you will always deliver. Try to get all the relevant data, information, facts, expert advice and clarity with regard to the crux of the matter before communicating with others. It will always give you extra impetus/mileage/advantage of being admired and an undisputed natural leader in the discussions.

Most of the people just for the sake of arguments come on the scene and without knowing the facts make the situation worse. In India, some of the self-proclaimed intellectuals give their opinions which are impractical and prescribe solutions which are dangerous than the basic problem itself.

Positive attitude is like icing on the cake, when the three parameters for positivity are in place in a person. Most of the people in this world have great fascination for negativity, saying a "BIG NO" is their DNA. They will find 1001 ways of not doing a work. They always want to be part of a problem rather than a solution. They never take decisions and let others take decisions. They have great respect for "Status Quo". They will always become wiser after the event is over. You will always find these people in your workplace, home, society lurking to pull down a good human being. These people will suck your time, energy and creativity by corrupting your mind with negative thoughts.

They may succeed sometimes but not always. The best way to find out such negative people is by their actions, they will never follow in life their own recommendations. Negative people follow Hit and Run policy.

The Question Is How To Deal With Such People?

The zeal to succeed in an adverse condition is positive attitude.

This cannot be imbibed or inserted in a person and by simply saying, I got positive attitude, will not do. What is to be seen is how a person converts failures and adverse situations in his favour. This requires a great deal of thought process, logical thinking and calmness. All those who have succeeded in life like Amitabh Bachan, Barrack Obama (US President), Steve Jobs, have demonstrated such skills. Never say die attitude and bouncing back from nowhere, is what makes a person positive. Great West Indies and Australian Cricket Team had shown this attitude in their prime. When the going gets tough then, Mr Tough gets going to define a positive person. You are the best judge of your situation and get your gut feeling and intuition strong with backing of reliable data. Some famous persons use intuitions or in some parleys known as obsessive compulsive disorders to get their actions hit the target. They try habitual things time and again to see that their future actions will be correct and get a proper frame of mind before going for the kill. This has nothing to do with positive attitude but it enhances confidence level of successful persons. Like Rafael Nadal puts on and off several shirts before going for the match and putting bottles in a particular fashion.

Positive people have the following three basic characteristics:

- Restlessness to get out of slumber
- Make their weakness as strength
- Always see the positive side of negative side. (Half glass as half full not as half empty)

There is a famous hindi movie saying ***"Har kar jitney waley ko bazigar kehatey hain."***

It means failure is the ladder for success. The people who come back from almost written-off are the real winners.

Synchronization and focused approach

"Synchronized and focused approach is the critical success factor for increasing the success rate."

Synchronized and focused approach are the critical success factors for increasing the success rate :

- Focusing on fewer tasks at a time.

- Re-align thinking to finish the activity on time instead of finishing tasks on time.
- Task prioritization rather than detailed schedules.

The above concept is used in project execution called the "Critical Chain" (CC) suggested by Dr Eli Goldratt which has been proven in increasing the rate of project execution by at least 20-30%. Synchronized and focussed approach helps in conflict resolution among stakeholders by focussing on the bigger issues of completing the project in time as a well-knit unit instead of competing with each other. Synchronization ensures timely decisions to mitigate uncertainty, while focussed approach will help in constantly looking for an opportunity to optimise the resources based on incremental benefits.

The idea here is to draw parity between the project execution concepts to managing life.

Three Precepts Of Critical Chain

PIPELINING: To limit the number of work-streams in execution, to reduce high work-in-progress (WIP), to concentrate resources on fewer streams of work at a time.

Parity

To achieve success, we have to plan things one at a time and try to prioritize the tasks and focus on the critical activity first to get the optimal results . Do not open too many fronts.

The failure of the AAP party, going for the Lok Sabha Elections without any planning, soon after the Delhi Elections is a classical example of opening too many fronts.

Buffering

Discard local schedules and measurements, and use aggregate buffers to protect against uncertainties. Instead of finishing tasks on time, focus on finishing the project on time. The final project deadline is the only deadline that really matters.

Parity

Try to look at the bigger picture and do not waste time on non-value added activities. Do not give much importance to negative things repeated. Objectives have to be focussed like Arjuna of Mahabharta and reassessed regularly.

Delhi Metro Rail Corporation (DMRC) Is A Live Example Of Such Success

Buffer Management

Instead of creating plans, focus on task prioritization - use the rate of project buffer consumption to measure execution, and give the highest priority to tasks that are consuming buffer at the fastest rate. Buffer-based priorities not only are synchronized, but they also cause project status to be reliable, giving managers actionable information they can use to focus resources on the tasks that are causing the biggest delays in project completion. Critical resources scheduling, its availability and optimisation are considered key performance indicators for a successful project management.

Parity

Try to utilize the leisure time in focusing and reassessing

the milestones in life and give thoughts regarding the catch up plans.

Most of the successful person in order to plan things to remain competitive use their leisure time when the mind remains in uncluttered fashion and helps them in creating fall back plans. Most of the crucial business decisions are sometimes taken by CEOs during golf playing sessions. They look things from different perspective which normally does not happen in a pressure cooked situation.

Time Management

"Buffer time is directly proportional to relative efficiency."

Like other resources, Time is also scarce. In business parleys or in general "Time saved is money saved". The person who factors changing time in his life will have success on sustainable basis. Managing time is the most difficult aspect in anybody's life as time flies. Time lost is opportunity lost. People always find themselves crying for having too much work-loads and time lines too harsh.

The middle class, try to enjoy life without creating opportunity for increasing their wealth. Family values are changing very fast. The degree of entropy (disorder) is increasing day by day, and if risk mitigation strategies are not applied in life, it will lead to unsuccessful life. The level of stress and fear of failure is killing the health of individuals.

The only thing can be done to stem the rot is Time Management. Do the following simple things in life, you will definitely say life is beautiful

- Plan next day's work in advance and be focused.
- Try to reach early in the office which will give you first mover advantage.
- Plan the daily work again. Sequence the activities/ work in a logical manner with maximum output.
- Try to eliminate the work early which requires less attention to reduce the work-streams.
- Try and orient the team towards finishing the jobs in the required time with a pep talk.
- Try to help the team when they are stuck or get help from your superiors.
- Relax, take deep breathes and talk to someone near and dear to relieve stress when you feel same is affecting your thoughts.
- Refresh with catch-up plan.
- Do not carry work at home unless it is very urgent.

This will enable you not only for your success at the professional front but also you will have enough time for leveraging quality time for family, pursuing your hobbies and also you can utilize the time saved for other activities like judicious use of your earned money by doing financial investments and leverage the same for your higher learning or acquiring skills which otherwise is a difficult preposition in current scenario.

Always remember your efficiency depends upon the efficiency of others. Unless you increase the efficiency of others, you will always have shortage of time. People have a tendency to play "waiting game syndrome". They play passing the pass without coordinating and resolving the issues. This waiting game has direct impact on your stress levels. Work stuck-up will eat away your leisure time and you will end up paying for the inefficiencies of others.

Buffer Time Is Directly Proportional To Relative Efficiency.

So how to do it :

- Rationalize the work-loads of the team from time to time based on their potential, skills, experiences and temperament being the most important.
- Induce boundary management skills in dealing with internal customers and team members.
- Be back benchers and let the team take the center-stage.
- Rationalize the appraisals and speak to each members personally to minimize heart burns.

There is a concept called EVM (Earned Value Management) in project management parleys to get buffer time intact.

- ➢ It is a way to measure the amount of work actually performed on a project.

- It is a way to forecast a project's cost and completion date using historical and statistical projections.
- It is a way to tell how well a project is "performing" compared to its original plan.
- Given this information it is a way to forecast how well the project will perform in the future.

In simple language or parity with life, it gives you where you stand today with regard to your work, how much more effort is required to reach your goal with scheduled time and cost. This will help you to analyze the situation better and help to focus on the critical activities and enable you to generate or keep the buffer time intact.

Suppose you have to travel a distance of 100 km in 5 hours with buffer time of 1 hour. After three hours you should cover as per plan 80 km, but you reach only 60 km, you are still 20 km behind the schedule. Now, for the balance 40 km to cover in 2 hours, how to have catch-up plan in place otherwise any slippage will not only eat away buffer time but cost of driving will also increase. It will have further cascading effect on your future scheduled work.

The idea here is to explain that time being the biggest constraint in life, is also the biggest healer if you have proper time management habits. Try to make time your companion and analyze your present, past and future with a close watch on the surroundings.

Human Touch Theory

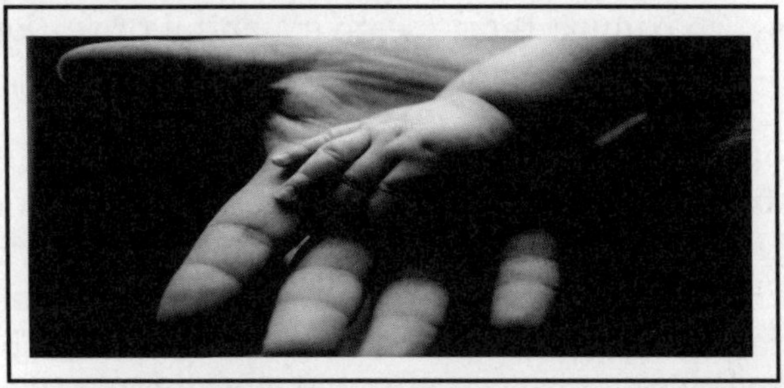

"Human touch theory means being concerned for the stakeholders especially people part."

We are increasingly becoming an anarchy society. Humans are no longer human. Humanity and Humility is being occupied by greed, selfishness, anxiety, stress, jealousy and hurt egos. Everybody thinks that he will be the last man standing, rest will die. A mad scramble for coming first is killing the Human Race. Make friends, avoid making enemies. Life is too short for wasting time on enemies. You never know goodwill leverage will help you grow. A simple word of encouragement or a tap at the back can help a small child do wonders, in case of seniors it multiplies.

Human touch theory means being concerned for the stakeholders especially people part. Word concern is very simple, but many companies/countries who have winning strike rate, become extinct only because they had shown little respect for the common people and talent of their work force. Profit oriented companies normally do not value human resources. They believe in retrenchment in a big way whenever their bottom–line gets hit. They never analyse the root cause of the problem but to remain competitive they choose the soft option. Great companies like Google, Microsoft value their Human Resources. Like it is said a family who eats lunch together, gel together and in the same way concern for the Soft part (People) in any organization brings the best out of individuals, help them to grow, maximize their creativity and in turn help the bottom-line of the organizations.

People are very judgmental today; they take everything on its face value and pronounce verdict even before it is actually out. We Indians have the habit of occupying the chair till our death or till somebody throw us out. Give space to younger generations, let them flourish. They are the future of our country; groom them with the right kind of values. The great example of the above idea is Indian Cricket team and Australian Cricket team. We find the stars of the Indian Cricket team always prolonged their careers to get maximum gains, whereas Australian Cricketer like Gilchrist who once said, the only competition I have got was with himself and left the stage for youngsters. In politics, also such scenario is common.

In work place, you will always find a person who is so called "Boss" sometimes bothers you. Some of the bosses have a feeling that they are the only Mr. Right in the world. Human Touch is a lost cause here. The reasons for such behavior are as follows:-

- They follow the same pattern which their predecessors have done to them.
- They do not want to share the power of decisions.
- They do not want to have overtake managers under them.
- They are individually brilliant but self-centric.

At a work place, such behaviour may create discord among the stakeholders which may lead to conflicts and heart burns, which is not good for health of the organization at large. The idea here is to have human touch theory in place and passing the relay batons to the subordinates in a dignified manner. Succession planning is an extremely useful tool to help manage the transfer and diffusion of knowledge within an organization. Knowledge, both tacit and codified, is one of the most important sources of competitive advantage in contemporary organizations. Additionally, succession planning can be used as a means to generate knowledge in order to achieve cost and operational efficiencies.

Simply passing the baton will not end in the desired result but empowering the people and their development is the key. Effectiveness of any planning should be seen in its execution. The idea is to choose the right candidate not just filling the positions. The organizations should do reality check from time to time with regard to talent pool. Empowering people will definitely induce the feeling of belongingness and it will reduce attrition rate at least at higher levels. Reward, recognition and loyalty bonus will also help in managing the talent.

Succession planning should be seen as risk mitigation strategy rather than as mere rituals. "Ego" is what is to be set aside and team work should be the theme.

In 2011, there was enormous concern about the success of Apple after Steve Job died. What saved Apple: An effective succession planning? The selection of leaders should not be limited to an individual but true succession planning breeds a culture that values talent, success and loyalty. Organizations looking to ensure management continuity should use diplomacy when approaching the current CEO about his or her impending retirement. Ultimately, it's in the CEO's best interest to ensure that the company lives long after his tenure. After all, nobody remembers the CEOs of dead companies. Have a vision, implement policies and systems that support that vision, and hire leaders and employees who reflect that vision. By doing that, they're building a company that will outlive any single CEO. And, that's a legacy anybody would be proud of.

A company can survive or sustain growth only when they have human touch theory in place by showing respect not only for their stakeholders but also for their competitors at large in order to have a mutual admiration society.

Information Assimilation and Dissemination

"Create `Aura' by marketing."

Today, information is available in abundance. The persons and companies who are successful and carries information about the environment will have an upper hand and share a first mover advantage. Time to market is the concept in today's business world based on Market Research. Media projection or frenzy created around a product, brand or a leader is what has been seen in the recent past as a success tool.

Such projections and faster information assimilation and dissemination determines the win-ability. The power of information is huge as people in today's world have a time constraint to analyze things, before coming to conclusions and mostly have herd mentality. Companies who have better product still are not able to sell as desired, only because they are not able to create an "Aura" behind their product in the minds of people.

Work smartly at your work place as hard work is always not saleable. Equip yourself with information, project yourself as natural leader and do not keep success of your team but disseminate and market the same to seniors. Many people, although they have great talent and business acumen than their peers, lost out in the race of top leadership because they have not created "Aura" for themselves.

The recent success of the AAP Party in Delhi was how media created "Aura" around Kejriwal as if he was the lone crusader against corruption or all the wrongs prevailing in our country. The likely failure of AAP has happened because these people were not well informed or they have not done their homework right. They were suffering from "A little knowledge is dangerous thing."

The success of honourable Prime Minister Shri Narendra Modi is about his projected developmental plans for India, however the same requires a concrete roadmap.

The idea here is to explain success based only on projection is not sustainable. What is required is to have information and data to back up those projections?

How to get the right information and how to disseminate the same to target audience

- Delphi Method: Asking Experts
- Historical Facts

- Market Information
- Brain Storming

Target audience is the critical success factor for getting recognized and winning admirers - How much to disseminate and when to disseminate ?

- Follow code of conduct or Professional and Business ethics in dealing with competitors.
- Filter the information before getting injected to target audiences.
- Do not hide anything critical with immediate bosses.
- Avoid Gold Plating in dealing with people at large.
- Try to rehearse before communicating.
- Seamless sharing of information with target audience.
- Clear and concise information with crux should be the motto.
- Make the discussions and communications interesting and appealing to the audience by making it as a story driven and crack some jokes having real life impetus.
- Try to elicit responses and involve stakeholders in decision making.
- Try to share information in a tabular form or with pictures, avoid using too many jargons.
- Sense the mood of stakeholders and time the information accordingly.

Right Kind of Environment

"Economic viability for a successful life."

China today is the world's driving force for the economy and will continue to do so. The environment in which we are in today belies all the belief that India will ever come closer to China. The idea of choosing this sub-topic is that "economic viability of successful life" especially of middle class is at stake today. Nuclear powered Pakistan is also a potential danger for Indian economy. Policies are mostly followed on an ad-hoc basis and sometimes ONLY a quid-pro-quo kind of decisions are being taken. Despite being put under BRIC countries (Brazil, Russia, India, China) as fastest emerging economies, India is now finding hard to keep its position. The idea of inclusive growth has taken a back seat. GDP growing at 8 percent on a consistent basis is a far cry as of now. The growth should be measured on Human Development Index and people purchasing power rather than solely on GDP figure. Although big companies like Tata, Infosys, Reliance and other Industries alike have got success on a sustainable basis and won, they are now feeling the pinch of so-called Policy Paralysis as mentioned by various leaders on various forums. Some people are winning today but India is not successful.

Is there any solution for the revival of Golden Era of

Bharat? Most people will answer in negative. Despite all the inherent problems, few basic things are suggested here—may be as tonic for the revival. Some of the so-called intellectual people will find these ideas repetitive but implementation of these simple ideas is a far cry.

- As it is said charity begins at top. Top leadership of this country is the key. Fragmented verdict in elections and `me first' attitude have killed decision making. Regional parties are sometimes playing spoil sport. Although they are representing regional aspirations, they should support the national parties contesting elections to have a stable government at the Centre and in turn get their pound of flesh for state development.

- People like Ambanis, Tata, Murthys and other experts/industrialists in consultation with RBI Governor and top leadership should pool their wisdom keeping aside bruised egos to make vision, mission and effective implementation to make "BHARAT" again. India first, should be the motto for such brain storming.

- Present systems should be made efficient rather then having more systems or mechanisms in place. We have to find solutions to a problem, rather than prescribe solutions which are more dangerous than the problem itself. This can only be achieved by making common people and persons giving services at the moment of truth as disciplined and accountable. Both top and bottom driven approach is required to stem the rot in the system. The Constitution adopted by India is a well thought one and excellent. The main area of concern today is that the people who are law makers, are themselves law breakers. Everybody is paid for doing a job, so why do we want more. The major reason is that the person believes that he has been paid less and want surplus to satisfy his family's materialistic needs. The only solution is reforms in a time-bound manner and zero tolerance for such demands.

- India's fiscal deficit may be huge but many people in India have fiscal surplus. Some call it black money. The best way to get such money is to allow people to voluntarily declare their assets within certain timeframe with the condition of 50% so-called black money amount will be returned back to them and rest will go to the Government in case they declare the same in stipulated time-frame. The money received will be used only for development of Infrastructures. This should be implemented without revealing the concerned person's identity. All the data like assets that a person has, driving license, pan card, passport, ration card etc should be one time entered in the UID card to make it effective rather than be an eyewash. This will not only give empowerment to the people of having all information captured at one place with updating facility but also prevent black money generation.

- India has to be self-sufficient so that prices of essential commodities should be within the reach of common people. Most of the developed countries have their food basket intact. In India, we still have to buy simple vegetable like onions and tomatoes from third world countries to meet the demand and beat the inflation. It is also a matter of shame that our farmers are dying due to hunger. Jai Jawan Jai Kisan (hailing the efforts of farmers and soldiers) is merely a slogan nowadays. Agriculture should be the main focus at least for the next few decades not only for self-sufficiency but also to improve the standard of living of villagers which will ultimately reduce their exodus from the villages. Make our farmers and jawans happy only then will India be happy.

- The most important thing today is to have a basic infrastructure. Look at China, the country has made huge strides in making Tier II and Tier III cities also on the economic horizons of the world. This has happened only by way of infrastructure like roads, electricity, law and order in place and maintaining the same with no room for complacency. This has resulted in better Human Development Index and People Purchasing Power in China. Poor planning and delayed implementation are the root cause of India lagging behind. During execution, local priorities set in, which overshadows the original project plan? It is like nobody knowing after all whose baby the project is and playing of waiting games begins.

Lessons learnt for completing such infrastructure projects

- *Selection of Project Manager*: A full time dedicated with proven track record Project Manager should be chosen, if required from outside the organization with no chopping and changing.

- *Selection of Project Team*: Create Heavy Weight team with personnel who are have past project experience, and are conflict resolver, team builder.

- *Autonomy for Decision-making and Conflict*

Management: This will help in resolving the issues and taking risks in the larger interest of project.

- *Change of Corporate Culture*: "We mean business" attitude is required.

- *Boundary Management*: Boundary management with all the stakeholders to ward-off any future problems.

- Above all *Top Leadership Commitment* is a must for the success of the project.

➢ Today, the Indian middle class intellectual is being tapped by the USA for the success/growth stories of their country. The best brains are working there as evident from the Satya Nadella appointed as the CEO of Microsoft. Why is such talent not working in India? In India, such talent and their ideas are not respected both in workplace or in social media or by Government at large while Companies like Google, Microsoft/Countries like USA know the importance of human intellectual power which has made them the knowledge center of the world. Today most of the MNCs are willing to work in India but a situation has been created called Policy Paralysis as normally referred in economic circles. The infighting among Political Parties to get bigger share of Power has made India a directionless country. Examine Business proposal of MNC by doing a cost benefit analysis with open mind and allow them to pump in money especially for infrastructure projects even if we fail to bring consensus. This will not only generate revenue, employment and provide stability to India's economic situation but also send message across the big players that India is serious.

- Today in the globalized world, we have to make risk sharing partnership with countries like USA, ASEAN group of countries, OPEC even if it is not on an equal footing. Indian economy is driven by fuels derived from Crude Oil. The price of Crude Oil is controlled by OPEC countries. No Government can do a jugglery and avoid inflation if prices of Crude Oil go beyond a threshold limit. Tax reforms will be of help on short term basis. The other option is to have long term pact with OPEC countries based on sharing each other's economies of scale for survival in the globalized market. China has shown the world what it takes to become an economic giant in a few years. China has leveraged their biggest asset-population and manpower to bring down cost of production. They have made other countries and companies partners for their growth. India having the same parameters like China but better intellectual hub, is still groping in dark. Here comes the role of leadership. Today, India is at the crossroads; anybody can jump on the media bandwagon and get limelight, create controversy and get noticed. Everybody in India seems to be leader in their own right and thinks that they have all the aces without consulting experts. Too many cooks spoil the broth. We require a man of substance who can act tough and make the system and people work. China is riding on tough leadership which has objective to go beyond the technological advance the western countries have made so far. No short term measures or quick fix solutions, policies and implementation should go hand in hand. Transparency and accountability should be paramount. Create environment for good governance. If leadership continues to show slackness on these accounts or do populist measures for short term gains, India will always come last. We have all the ingredients and resources to make a meal which will be tastier to all the stakeholders. What is required is commitment like DMRC to make everybody winner not a few as exists today. It's a challenge which China accepted in the 90s with same conditions India has today. **"Hum honge kamyab ek din—should be the motto."** (Means- Yes we will succeed one day, Like Barrack Obama Slogan, Yes We Can). The resolve is not to have the numbers or statistics on our platter but the real benefits derived by having our basics in place. Winners do not take it all; the losers have all the reasons to smile to get better of the winners. To have sustainable growth, we have to work with our economic structure rather than coping from the western countries. India is a difficult country to manage with diverse mind sets. Today the youth of all castes and religions want job for their survival, the leadership has to create environment by allowing industries to grow and provide infrastructure on Private-Public models. The idea here is to make Tier II and Tier III cities capable enough to generate employment. People should work for stability of the future generation, otherwise a hostile China will laugh all the way. Proper planning with meticulous execution is the key for success.

Part-2

Self and Country Winning

Mainly related to self and country success coupled with more real life backings and solutions oriented to make the winning count.

Hiring Dilemma

"Whom will you prefer to be hired for your Company or want in your team?"

Sachin vs Rahul

The vital statistics of above contenders are as follows:

Sachin

1. Great reputation of being a brilliant individual.
2. Lacks leadership qualities as being somewhat self-centric.
3. I am okay and failures are for the team members to share.
4. Takes bigger share of the pie being regarded as an outstanding performer.
5. Strike rate of getting the bottom line hit, on an average is around 60-70%.

Rahul

1. Great reputation of being consistent and finisher.
2. Shown leadership qualities. Takes extra responsibilities.
3. Takes failures as stepping stone and regroups the team.
4. Allows team to take a bigger share of the pie.
5. Strike rate of getting the bottom line hit, on an average is around 80-90%.

India or companies today require a team of finishers or leaders who work on back stage with finesse rather than individual brilliance to remain competitive. The joy of collective brilliance can be shared without any heart burns. The great Australian Cricket team of 1996 onwards and West–Indies team of 70's-80's are the examples of success / failure being enjoyed by everybody which proves winning is not always success. What is required is to have a healthy environment for self-competition to improve the bottom-line. Individual brilliance can take you at certain level only but not always, collective wisdom of team will generate out of box things which will provide you the cutting edge.

A recent development in many reputed companies like Infosys has again reinforced the idea of having succession planning in place. The stakeholders who are restless are closely watching such developments. The leadership issue at various levels in the organization should be open-ended and real thought process is required to have a candidate who has the vision and mission to carry the organization forward. It is one of the greatest challenges for the organizations for their sustenance to have the right candidate selected. The set of skills has to be defined upfront for the creation of talent pool. A few people in the organization running the show are not only individually brilliant but they are self-centric in their approach. They never share their tacit knowledge in order to enjoy their supremacy. You may be a gold medalist, but it is the duty of the senior management to create silver medalists within the organizations. This will not only increase the self-esteem of the employee who will be groomed for the future role but also help the organization to retain talent. This means winning is not always important it is the belongingness and people who identify themselves with the company or country that means success. The bottom line should not mean only profit but creation of wealth for the stakeholders at large.

And the winner is--

Author's take

We require both Rahul and Sachin in the team but more

of Rahul. In the PMI Conference at Gurgaon, CEO of `Make My Trip', Mr. Deep Kalra , during his speech clearly told that they require people who work for them rather work for themselves. Today, companies who are working on smaller margins are hesitant in hiring IIT and IIM graduates as some of them play spoil sport being egoist and do not relish working in a team. After you acquire hard skills, your soft skills determine your success rate. Be a team man, you will definitely get bigger share of pie for your extraordinary skills.

Positivity vs Negativity

Too much Positivity without objectivity laden with arrogance (not accommodating other views); hurt Egos, breeds negativity.

This is what we are fast becoming. The classical example of today's India is the AAP Party Chief—Arvind Kejriwal. We must congratulate him and the Anna Movement to bring the issue of corruption in the limelight. The various scams have taken some sheen out of India's GDP growth stories and I in BRIC, regarded as one of the fastest growing economies ALREADY gone.

The AAP Party started with a positive mission and full support from people of all walks of life which was reflected in Delhi's Assembly elections. Arrogance had led to the failure of Anna Movement and same is now taking toll on Aam Aadmi Party. The manner or speed of arrogance with which Arvind Kejriwal is moving, it will fast become a single man party (Akela Aadmi Party-means One Man Party). Bullying tactics, objective lost, credibility on wane is what Aam Aadmi Party is getting into it. It is hard to break the rotten system, but the ways and means to break the same adopted by Shri Arvind Kejriwal team was a lot to be desired. My way is no way. What we are witnessing todays is to grab power at any cost. He had pressed the self-destructive button like Bhasmasura in Hindu Mythology who got a wish from Shiva to destroy any body on which he could place his hand on the head. He finally died by being made to put his hand on his head.

Whether Arvind Kejriwal is successful? The concept of positivity say NO. Arvind Kejriwal has the opportunity lost but he can still prove critics wrong by focusing on fewer tasks. Success is what you indulge in by getting the lives of people better. All those people who work tirelessly like E Sreedharan, V J Kurien, APJ Abdul Kalam with single focused objective have their action plan, task force worked out, and are the real winners.

I will just quote one famous story from the *Mahabharta* which finally lead to the war between the Kauravas and Pandvas which clearly shows how hurt egos are disasters.

One day Duryodhan the son of blind King Dhritrastra visited Indraprastha Palace (newly constructed residence for Pandavas) out of curiosity to see the creativity and magical touch it breeds. He in his enthusiasm put his wrong foot forward in an illusion which actually was a pond. He fell into the pond and Draupadi, wife of Pandavas started laughing at him. She remarked "*Andhey ka beta Andha*" (Blind son of a blind father). This hurt the ego of Duryodhana and he vowed to take revenge. He asked Yudhistra to play chausar (a kind of chess) and Yudishtra lost his wife Draupdi in a gamble. He molested Draupadi in front of everybody. This incident finally led to a war in Kurukshetra and ultimately started the yuga of Kalyug (era full of dishonesty, cheating, mistrust, distrust, backstabbing which is still prevalent). The lesson learnt is that we should be careful in our judgment and choose words to win friends to avoid hurt egos. Today you find people are doing just the opposite to that to get mileage and false pridehood.

Saas-Bahu (Mother-in-law and bride fight) serials and Political Debate on the Indian TV screen will give you all the ingredients for negativity. Arvind Kejriwal has become the toast of today's politics for his contradictory statements and actions (His antics are now being called as drama by media) while the issue of corruption has gone for a toss once again.

Negativity personified people galore and you need not have to go to the market to shop these types of people. This is the only commodity where Supply is more than the Demand always. These people wisdom will not only slow down the progress but also cause damage beyond repair.

Test or probability for finding people with negativity or positivity skills: Ask them to draw a figure of snake. However I do not have any scientific reason for this.

Positivity or negativity skills are directly proportional to the head of snake drawn above the ground level.

A person will have more probability of having positivity skills if he draws a snake with a head much above the ground. A major chunk of a negative skill will always draw snake's crawling or will draw the head of the snake just above the ground level.

Negativity or fear of rejection is the way of life for the Indian middle class and that is why we do not have any out of the box thinking. We want to remain like as per the Hindi saying "Kueny ka mendahk" (Frog in Pond believe the world is not beyond his pond) Or Lizard Syndrome (believing that we are only holding the fort) and accordingly factored in enough safety cushion in our approach which prevents us to go beyond a certain level.

My wife, like in most of the homes, is my biggest critic. As I am not carrying any surname, she calls me Abhinav JD (Jani Dushman- Means Bad Blood). She will always keep me busy even if you are some sort of achiever in your life (Ghar ki murgi dal barabbar- Means Useless fellow). We have to look into the aspect whether the criticism is adding value (Positive Criticism) or eroding value (Negative Criticism) to your life, a kind of trade-off is required. In case of relatives, 90% time it falls in the latter category, because of intense rivalry syndrome, more than your non-blood relations. No doubt, relatives are helpful but they will keep you low when you are down. All kind of useless stuffs, they will prescribe as if they are the sole bearer of your problem (*Aag mein ghee ka kaam karna or Jaley pe namak chhidakna*- Means Adding fuel to the fire or rubbing salt on your wounds). The problem starts when such repeated negative suggestions get into your mind and wrong decisions are being made. Please remember you are the sole judge of your problem, take or implement advises judiciously, ultimately you will be the sufferer. I remember, somebody advised his cousin to join Guwahati IIT (Computer Science) instead of Mechanical at IIT, Delhi. All of us know that Guwahati being new IIT does not have the matured faculty for such courses. The end result, the cousin did not get a lucrative job. However, in case of their own son, they will do the opposite. We should guard against Manthras of this world. (Manthra, the maid servant, was the famous character in Ramayana who instigated Kaikayee, one of the queens of King Dhasarath to get his son Bharat as king in place of Lord Rama).

Now coming to my wife, the problem or negativity starts when she starts downplay your success or you down playing her success. Comparison with others is not advisable. If the criticism is skewed towards more negativity or guided by some relatives advices, then it will boil down to wire. The best way to salvage the situation is by saying "Sorry" to each other and with a cool head to resolve the situations with facts and figures rather than shouting on top of voice to get the winning pole position.

Every house has its own complexity but there are certain human behaviors common across the board. Your friends, foes or wife may not be your soul-mate but what is required is mutual respect. The idea here is not to have upmanship but to get things in the right perspective for the sake of our own children who are the real causality of such intolerance. Winning such situations is in fact losing.

Please note that Kalidasa, a famous poet of ancient India became a great writer once he got ridiculed by his wife as he was not up to the mark by his wife's standard, so either you become a great poet making your worth count or face the reality of life with a zeal to succeed.

We all want to be understood. Use shift key on the computer to move from being understood to understanding?

Otherwise we will have bruised egos. Understand that we don't always understand each other. Understand that we're different in our abilities.

Approach others with understanding and you open the door to being understood. My mobile does not have the phone number saved of my wife, whenever I have to call, I type, just to delay the firing for a few seconds.

Personal Success Concept

LEARN TO GROW AND GROW TO LEARN (IT IS LIKE THE FAMOUS HINDI MOVIE TITLED LAGEY RAHO MUNNA BHAI NEVER GIVE UP LEARNING)

After completing 12th Class, it is up to the individual to decide what they want to achieve in their life. It is the most crucial phase of anybody's career. In India due to non-support from Government for getting success in other fields and under family pressure, middle class objective is skewed towards studies. MBA/MCA/Engineers/CA/Doctors are a few chosen disciplines. Most prefer being Engineers/MBA among the present youth to have killer combo in their kitty. But you can always follow your passion.

Today your personal success is determined by the skills set or academic qualifications or achievements you have in your kitty. The following basic tips needs to be followed to get you some academic success to get head start in your life which is based on effort you put after 10th class

1. Get the fundamentals or basic concepts cleared instead of cramming.

2. Do regular studies and practice the concepts. Make your 11th standard time count, as student become complacent after 10th and distractions happens due to the inherent biological changes (Love is in the air).

3. Do not bother about not getting into a premier Institute. Get into decent one.

4. Work hard during your professional degree. (Facebook / Google are looking for talent as one of the student from MNR, Allahabad got the highest package, not chosen from IIT, Satya Nadella—Current CEO of Microsoft is from Manipal institute).

5. Most importantly, PARENTS play an important role in counseling the child, so be behind them in the event of success and failure, after all you have worked hard with your child in their upbringing and nothing is more important than your pampered child's journey for life. Avoid partying and social meetings on a regular basis at least for the two crucial years 11th and 12th of your child to keep the focus going.

First job is like First love. When you get into the job, the job specification and description for the post remain same for everybody.

Personal skill sets, more degrees, work experience which makes package higher for the same post as compared to others. You need not to worry? Be a *"lambi race ka Ghoda"*- Means—Hard work and perseverance will take you to the greater heights. Work for some time in the organization and get the feel of nuances of working. You have two options: leave the job or remain in the job in order to get more professional degree like MBA/LAW/CA/Job related higher skills in your kitty. The various CEO's of many big companies have already realized the concept of "Learn more and earn more", that's why they are there at the top and which enables to the successful professionals to climb up the ladder faster than others. Continue your learning skills for repeated success.

Now we can talk about the soft skills OR acumen to sustain success. People are chosen for a job based on hard skills but their soft skills make all the difference.

Work experience is a learning curve. Some of the soft skills or acumen learning, we get from training or doing some course as mentioned above and some we get by experience or lessons learnt, but we never implement those, because we feel we know everything. Change is for others to follow. Try to reinvent yourself, be a change manager for your organization, and groom yourself for future leadership role. Your acumen, boundary management skills, success build on lessons learnt and response time in accumulating and disseminating information will help you to grow.

N R Narayana Murthy when he retired from Infosys in 2011 had said "It's a dream team, I'm leaving it in safe hands". He was referring in particular to K V Kamath, his successor in the Chairman's position, Kris Gopalakrishnan, the executive co-chairman, and S D Shibulal, CEO & MD. However Mr. Shibulal had fallen short in his expectations as N R Narayana Murthy returned to the helm again. The reason he failed was because he did not realize the power of soft skills.

Home Success Concept

Are you enjoying the little things in your life?

Today, in the fast paced world with various pulls and pressures both at home and work front, is taking a heavy toll on our health. Keeping family and job intact is a major challenge today. Today most of middle class are fast becoming a community of DIG (Double Income Group). Work pressure's biggest causality is quality life. The formulae for success both at home and work front on a continuous basis is not trying to score a point or two always for the sake of winning or arguments but to get your smile back. Check your health status first, increase in the population of grey hair, weird look, irritating behaviour, not enjoying the meal, no sound sleep for even 2-3 hours, not able to say customary hello to your loved ones, man you are heading for disaster. The live example which came to light recently was the death of Ranjan Das, CEO and MD of SAP Indian subcontinent (One of the youngest CEOs, he was 42) died after a massive cardiac arrest. The reason for his sudden demise was lack of sleep and his strenuous regime of fitness. He himself said that he would love to get more sleep and that he was not proud of his ability to manage without sleep. In this self-centric world, you will be left licking your wounds, so please note that health is your triumph card for success. Please note that you will be the sole bearer of hypertension, diabetes, depression or other health problems. So, do not push your body too much, otherwise body will start reacting and share your feelings with your true well wishers who will give you a patient hearing.

Here Just I say one line from the famous Urdu song

Seeney mein jalan, akhoon mein toofan sa kyon hai, Ish Seher mein har Saksh pareshan sa kyon hain

It means the hectic life has snatched away our happiness and our basket is full of angst, stress, depression, and health related problems. Everybody is trying to win by hitting six on the last ball and trying hard to get noticed under distress.

The concept of Incremental approach with added value will do wonders to your success. As the company's margins are getting thinner and thinner, they work on this concept.

This is the same as Value Chain by Porter Model

The Porters Value Chain model distinguishes between primary activities and support activities as shown below. The firm must examine all the process or activity which adds value to its product or service. If the process does not add value, then the firm will revamp the process, eliminate the process or outsource so that the same contributes to the bottom line.

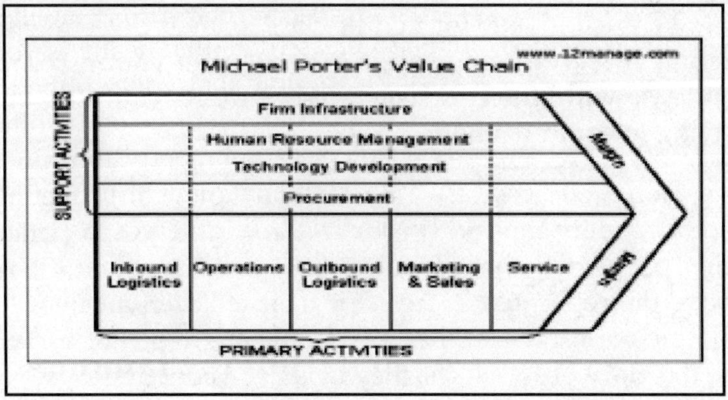

You may be a good quality manager in your organization but at home you never check the processes required to get your home bottom line hit. The incremental approach will give you a clear picture and make you analyze the things better.

Priorities drastically change when you become parents. This is the time when you have no time and life becomes real game changer. Real test of character is required. Time-line and targets at office and parenthood goes hand in hand. Do not force through the problems but try to take things in your stride and do not over-react. Try to be a good listener and talk to every stakeholder in the house including your servant to have a holistic approach to *Sass-Bahu, Naukar-Malik,* Children–Parents conflicts, otherwise you will be gone for a toss.

It is like Urdu shayari " *Aur bhi gamm hain jindagi mein mohabaat ke siva*". It means life is full of tragedies, we have no time for love.

Financial security is the key for the future of the Indian middle class and home success. Earlier, people had mindsets in keeping the money in the bank and afraid of investments. You have to decide whether the money in the bank is adding any value to your future generations. Try to invest to get the money multiplied. The safe option for hard earned money for middle class today is investment in home. It serves two purpose—the value of your asset will increase with due course and also it meets your dream of living in your own house.

Home success also depends on how you devote or spend quality time with your children. You will invariably find people who have made a name for themselves, do not have the replicated success for their children always. The simple reason is that they are deeply engrossed or basking in the glory of successes, they never consider family as part of their success. Here the natural succession phenomenon works, which makes their children non-creative some times.

Are their winning always a success? Answer is NO. The joy one can get seeing their children making a mark on the world or challenging the world on their own will always be cherished. People judge a person's win-ability not only on his personal success but also on how he gets his family along the success path. We can always take pride in our children's success rather than on our personal success and hence, who ever does that is the real winner.

I will explain the concept with a real life example of myself being in the thick of things.

During the first four-five years of our service, we focused on savings and essential expenditure only. This has enabled us to realize our first house with bank loan. Realizing the potential of real estate, we invested our saved money again in second house. There was great opposition from relatives to keep the money in the bank but we made them understand that this will be an opportunity lost. The idea here is simple when you climb up the ladder you have to see what value-add you are delivering to your children for their future. You need not have to run after the money, it is the judicious use of hard earned money that makes for your home success.

Follow simple steps while investing in Homes

- Never follow anybody's advice, verify yourself; after all it is your hard earned money. Your investment will cause loss if the money is blocked for more than 5 years in the project.

- Take time-off your schedule and take a round of the locations where you want to invest. Please enquire about the development of the location in near future with Authorities.

- Interact with the three or four reputed builders. Negotiate with them.

- Examine their proposals and expected time line for completion of the project. Most important is to look for penalty clause in the proposal.
- Do a cost-benefit analysis between investment and completion of project.
- The most important is to check the proven track or past record of builders and also how many projects they have right now in their hand. Also important are the penalty clauses for delay he is offering.
- Most important of all, please check whether the project is being financed by leading banks of India, so that you can verify all the necessary approval from authorities that are in the builders backyard.
- Never invest in project which has residential, mall, hospitals kind of concept. Please invest only in residential projects for timely return of your money.
- Get the loan on fixed rate preferably from the bank which approved the project as the floating rate fluctuates now a days too much.
- Please note that a rupee worth today is more than Rupee tomorrow (Time value for money). So start early in investing in your career so that the money of 30-40 lacs will buy today 3 BHK but investing the same money at a much later stage of career will fetch you a 2 BHK in the same location. And also starting early will smoothen the pinch of EMI at a later stage.
- Also, if feasible, get a MOU signed by a group of people with builders to get quantity discount. It is like an old saying in hindi "*Dubengey sanam to sabko*

sath lekey dubengey". It means we have to make risk sharing partners.

Another challenge faced by parents today is children's studies. Today the level of distraction is paramount for children and studies require a lot of mental effort and patience than any other activity. That is why most people successful in other fields have somewhat limited success with academics. Study is the bread and butter of the middle class in India. Although we have talent to become famous or can do great things by following our passions, but the harsh reality is that we do not have luxury to go beyond studies for a better or a sustainable life. Success rate in risk taking is challenging and demanding as shown by many successful persons in their field, but all people are not risk savvy, for them, survival is the key. Here I am not desisting people to follow their passions and become great, but only suggesting to be realistic based on their potential and reality of a mad world.

Just follow the following tips to get the child going:

- Try to get the fundamentals or concept right during the first five- six years of schooling and encourage them to participate in extra–curricular activities to get their creativity out. Please remember, today most schools normally crave for marks rather than on child special skills.

- Do not force the child for marks, try to analyze his mistakes and guide him during his early years.

- Keep focus on his/her studies and make them understand that studies are equally important along with their passions.

- Encourage the idea of self-study and regular study rather than forced study.
- Try to change gears after the child achieves a level of understanding for challenging him/her with high order thinking skills.
- Practice is the key.
- Get the child to have a decent day out on some Sundays and Saturdays to relieve the stress. Make summer vacations utilized for practical learning to groom them for a complete personality.

Please note that success of your child is your success and effort. It is also notable that the child who performs better in studies also performs or succeeds in delivering the knockout punch in life or will have their passion as success in some point of time. Learning the hard way is the only way for success, whatever you do in your life.

Soon after the birth of my second child; I was transferred to Panipat from Delhi after 11 years from pure office work to real action work at the plant. The distance of 260 kms roundtrip was the real challenge. No luxury or leisure time now, daughter's study requires attention, wife being working requires moral support, managing finances, work pressure at office increased thrice.

I will explain how incremental approach had helped me in dealing with the above problems

Distance

It involves both money and time constraint and physical stress even if you commute at least 2 days a week after a hard day's work. Immediately I bought a diesel car. I have made the distance covered in phases or milestone-wise to remove the mental block. Tried to maximize the speed when the road was free in order to meet the target of 2½ hours in reaching the destination. Most important, listening and singing to the melodious songs of 70s and 90s which took care of some of my time and physical stress. I maximize the speed on highway and tried to refresh the mind after reaching at a particular milestone, (Incremental approach) considering the same as the new starting level. My wife's colleagues had quoted I should be given the Bravery Award during the Republic day along with various awardees for managing the home front as well. Here the challenge was not reaching in time but the hall mark of success was how to reach safely in time.

Managing the show at home

The most difficult part for me was my daughter's studies which was suffering as I was the first person responsible. Every week the school had Unit Tests and I have Saturday and Sunday to have my battery recharged and get a deep peep into her studies. The moment of truth comes when baby wanted his pound of flesh, wife and mother wanted. Their objectivity of daughter's studies had taken a back seat. Activity takes time and I have to cut non-value added activities and innovate every now and then to squeeze time. First and most important thing to get your nerves calmed. Eliminate the process OR activity like watching TV, try to do parallel activities like taking snack and tea along with daughter studies, make her charged-up before-coming. We try complex thing but forget to do small things (Eliminate non-value adds) is what is required to get the things done within a time constraint.

Success at Work

Being a Procurement manager, my work load at Panipat Naptha Complex, increased many a times, as the plant is purely based on procurement of inputs. The supplier base is too thin and that too inputs are imported and getting inputs timely delivered is a major challenge to prevent production loss without building inventories too much. No second chance in contrast to Indian Cricket, where people get a life-line several times despite repeated failures and some continue to enjoy luxury being a non-performer or having an average winning strike rate due to *Boss ka Chamcha Syndrome*- Means Proximity with Boss. We have to be on our toes all the time and have to hit sixes and fours only. I employed my leisure time at home or work or when I have little distractions to get the work planned in advance. (Plan before plan to have incremental approach workable or value added). Attack the lesser time consuming but important jobs first. Keep all the stakeholders apprised of the situations to get the maximum out of them. The most important is to keep smiling. It is like a dead man walking but smiling seeing the work done as planned or even if the situation worsens. A little joke cracked; talk about politics, or sharing any boss bashing with the team will get you the fatigued engine working (Value add to your health).

Please note that after some time your work success is primarily dependent on your home success but not vice-versa.

Some people will say what is great in this; success is not what you achieve once or twice, what is required is to have consistency in life and enjoying little things in life which is the most difficult paradox in today's fast paced world.

Family Values vs Society Success

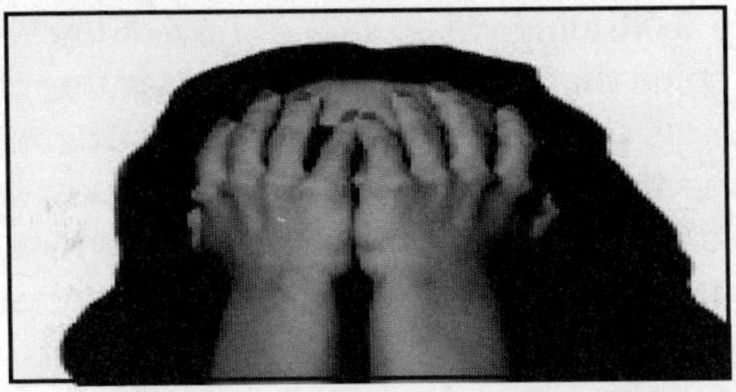

"Are we fast becoming an insane society?"

Culture of insanity has engulfed both family and society which has led to the degeneration of our moral values. Today we are fast becoming a society of pretention with a sadistic attitude. We never enjoy the success of others but dig deep into other's failures. There is one famous dialogue in the Hindi Movie "Three Idiots" that our result in examination does not matter most but we drive solace only when by seeing the result of your best friend less than yours.

We still remember the famous case of the kidnaping and killing of Geeta and Sanjay Chopra by two young men, Ranga and Billa. The entire nation was outraged. However, the situation has changed since then. The recent case of Nirbhaya which was made counted only when media intervened and murders of senior citizens in Delhi are the glaring reflection of our fragmented society today. We only react when we get hurt. We have increasingly become a soft society.

Family values and society success are the two sides of the same coin. What we learn at home gets reflected in society and the other way around also. However success at home does not mean you will be perceived as a successful person for the society or vice versa.

Today materialistic attachment has replaced natural attachment. We have made ourselves sealed in air tight compartments and do not want to come out of our comfort zones. The technological advances have somewhat ruined our life to enjoy the natural surroundings rather than having virtual friends on the social networking sites. Addiction to such sites is the major area of concern today, as children have access to all kinds of stuff available at their doorsteps. Children are getting away from the parent supervision and becoming more recluse in their approach. The recent incidents of shootout by the recluse young children in their school in the USA has resulted in the loss of many innocent lives, MMS scandals, unhealthy relationships leading to suicides and many more side effects which are the pitfalls of such addiction.

So where is the flaw?

Flaw is our insanity. We do not pay attention or turn a blind eye or become ostrich and have the motto that "All is Well" as we consider these events as self-correcting and self-inflicting. Greed for more is the root cause of such insanity which is making moral and ethics irrelevant. In the quest of beating others we are beating ourselves in the long run. There is one small story in which a person is having a hen which gives him daily one golden egg. In the quest for more, he decides to cut the hen to get all the eggs in one go and end up getting nothing. Today the same fate is happening to the cricket, which we love and play. IPL is just symbolic of the downfall of moral and ethics in our society. Players are the hen here whose body is being abused as they play cricket almost 360 days in a year and still continue to be used by money mongers, making the passion or love for the cricket irrelevant.

In the micro nuclear family today, without any *Dada*

and *Dadi* or *Nana* or *Nani* (Grandparents) living in the same house, probability of children going the wrong way increases. As working parents do not have sufficient time for their kids, children in such family are likely to suffer from low moral and family values, insensitivity and aggressiveness in their approach and indulge themselves in bad habits. Today, parents absolve themselves of all responsibilities of parenthood by providing all the materialistic things to their children.

It is a wake-up call for all of us to make our family bonding strong to have a better society. Also we should desist from playing dirty politics in the societal circles which perpetuates hatred and non-performance.

The best parents/children/societal groups can do under these circumstances is to foster culture of values which are the backbone for the success of family and society

1. Be human. At least react to the non-human acts.

2. Have respect for elders. At least say *namastey* (wishes) to them.

3. Parents should have respect and concern for each other. This is very important considering the increase in divorce cases. And also, for the psyche of children who finally bear the brunt of such separations.

4. Children should take guidance from their elders regularly to beat the pressure of academics or expectations and try to be honest with themselves. Never hide anything unusual before it is too late. Problems can only be solved by discussions. Remember, Parents are the best friends.

5. At least eat one meal together for enriching the bonding.

6. Societal groups should organize events in their vicinity to foster confidence building measures like rewarding any successful person, competitions for children, celebrating festivals or any milestones in their area by keeping politics or supremacy out of it.

7. People should make the MLA/MP/MLC of their area accountable for carrying developmental activities.

Here family is the key, where you can exercise some control. Womanhood has to be respected. Mother's behaviour emanates a child's initial mental frame set up. Mother is the best person to get the family values and moral values embedded in a child. We should salute the woman for their different roles they perform with finesse and help the societal values to flourish. Today, crime against woman has increased considerably which represents the degeneration of our value system. Woman who cares for us should be cared and appreciated. Stringent and rational laws should be made so that it can be implemented without trivializing the issues related to woman. Modern woman should look forward to getting economically sound themselves and should emulate or idolize successful ladies like Ms. Indra Nyoi, Pepsi Chief ; Ms. Chanda Kochar, ICICI CEO to challenge the regressive society. Woman liberation lies in recognizing their inner self rather than going ballistic for the materialistic things. American or Western society is the live example of fall out of family values due to non-commitment to marriages and affection for materialistic things. The recent Hindi movie "Queen" which is a kind of self-discovery for woman should be seen as liberation from clutches of bad Indian mentality of keeping their self-esteem low but not at the cost of being woman.

The only take away for making the Moral and Family Values intact and have a healthy and progressive society in today's world is to "Keep your family intact and SOCIETY should show respect for woman who are the saviour of the human race"

Implementation of Projects

DMRC Vs Commonwealth Games

A quick look at the delayed projects indicates "failure in resolving associated issues of local priorities during execution" as the prime reason for project overruns. The issues may be diversion of resources allocated for a specific work, delay in issuance of work-permits etc. At ground zero, indecision galore as managers afraid of being targeted try to build in more time lag for their activities and play waiting games by blaming others for their misfortunes instead of synchronizing and focusing on completing the task in a proactive manner. This ultimately has a cascading effect on the project timeline.

The following are the major areas wherein indecision occurs which gives headache to Managers and ultimately lead to delays :-

1. Technical Area

    - Scope change;

- Engineering and design change
- Material requirement planning

2. Financial Area

- Improper estimation
- Statutory risks

3. Organizational Area

- Too many decision makers/conflicts
- Contractors failure
- Suppliers failure
- External pressure

The factor `scope change' has been identified as the most vulnerable for the project as it has high probability of occurrence as well as high severity. If there is a change in scope of any of the work packages, there will be considerable implications on design, planning and implementation program. These will cause considerable time and cost overrun in project. Implementation methodology, fund risk, improper estimate and materials risk are rated as medium with respect to probability of their occurrence as well as severity. The factors like land acquisition, technology selection, engineering and design change, contractor's capability, vendor's capability and abnormal calamity are also rated as medium probability but with less severity, as adequate planning for the project under study prompts the executives to perceive these factors as less vulnerable. However, project will experience major time and cost overrun, if any of the above factors occur during project implementation.

Most of the capital intensive projects, got delayed due to multiple changes in scope, design & engineering. This is mostly attributed to insufficient research/ground work done in execution related issues by OWNER/PMC (Project Management Consultant) during detailed planning which leading to improper estimation of job/scope, work packages not well defined and improper scheduling. This causes heartburn at the execution time with fronts not available to contractors, rerouting of the process line and more Material Take off (MTO). This will finally result into resources not being available or idling of Contractor resources. The situation gets more compounded with delay in getting change orders approval from top management (too many decision makers).

Commonwealth Games were deprived of Governmental support. Everybody was heading the Commonwealth Games in his own right, right hand did not know what left hand was doing. We have a habit of keeping things pending and lay back attitude till it becomes critical.

Lack of accountability, governance and risk mitigating strategies as evident from the fiasco of Commonwealth Games 2010 brings the two invaluable facets of Project Management, Project Governance and project Risk Management, at the forefront. The role of project governance is to provide a decision making framework that is logical, robust and repeatable to govern an organization's capital investments while the role of risk management helps the professionals to recognize the benefits of formally documenting, objectively analyzing and transparently managing risk.

Success of any project depends on how you manage "soft part" (People) of project, "autonomy" for decision and "greater zeal" to achieve the target: what exactly is shown in the DMRC Project.

"The successful implementation of the Delhi Metro project would not have been possible without timely availability of funds and the necessary political support. An equally important role has been played by the DMRC's corporate culture, which emphasizes that targets are most sacrosanct and our dignity is in performing our duty well." - E. Sreedharan, Ex-MD , DMRC.

A synchronized and focused approach is a game changer for managing complex projects and ensures timely payback.

Projects especially infrastructure are the key for India's growth. Today winners take it all, the development stories are not percolated down the lane is what is taking India on the back foot. Measurable benefits not mere statistics will decide outcome as success.

Past vs Present

India got freedom 70 years back and it still has not realized its full potential.

Has India actually got freedom?

We are fast becoming a society of self-centric people. "*Jugaad* and *sab chalta hai* culture (Means we can fix everything and every non-sense thing around us is okay) is the order of the day". Our Constitution was made with all good intentions and we have made a mockery of the same today. We have all become critical of the system but never complained when the self-job was being done by unfair means.

Selfless was the key, `India first' was the motto when the Indian democratic set up began. The challenges today are far more challenging than what we had earlier and with passage of time it will further become grave. Population vs Resources imbalance is the main hurdle in reaching the break-even point and wiping off the fiscal deficit.

In post Independence era, what Sardar Patel had achieved was remarkable, getting the fighting kings and diverse culture of Bharat united in one umbrella called India. But today what we are finding is the reverse and people are ignoring India and fighting for their regional aspirations. It is simple if India's GDP improves, it will benefit the entire population. But the delivery system is so rotten; the development benefits does not reach down the lane and this anomaly is causing heart burns. Though the Britishers have looted Indian wealth but they had left the trail and foot prints of development on which our rebuilding process started post-independence. Today some of the masters have become looters with the main objective to further their future. Basic things like education, electricity, sanitation, roads, housing are still a far cry in Today's India. Most of the poor people are still living in worst condition as in pre Independence India.

Green or Milk revolution which was run by the ordinary common people of India and now IT, Space, Metro revolution or others run by the talented Middle class of India are the success stories which has restored India's Credibility. Tough Leadership Skills which was shown by Late Smt. Indira Gandhi during the Pakistan War and also the financial reforms done during Late Narshimha Rao Government with our back on the wall were commendable.

Today India is being run on self-inflicting and self-correcting basis. Let us begin operation / Project *"Bharat Vijai Bhavo"*(Means - Make India Win). We, today, are having Prime Ministerial Candidates in abundance. The questions remain whether they have the right project proposal to turn it around for India. The project proposal should include a time bound programme in place with effective implementation strategy. They should publish the project proposal in writing as happened in American elections to let people know broadly how they will be generating revenues and curtailing the expenditure rather just publishing manifestoes.

To get the project monitored, we must have a PMO (Project Management Office) for *Bharat Vijai Bhavo* project, with genuine experts in their respective field along with project management professionals unlike the PMO office attached with the Prime Minister who will provide all the support mechanisms and resources in a co-ordinated manner to get the job done and obstacles removed at the grassroot level.

The project proposal broadly should include the following which is a very important document in Project Management to start a project (for more knowledge and related guideline on Project Management, please read PMBOK Guide issued by PMI, USA):-

1. **Project Name-***Bharat Vijai Bhavo* (Require feasibility studies by experts)

2. **Project Objective-**To make India a self-reliant and true growth oriented country on sustainable basis by the next 10 years with fruits of development reaches to the poor.

3. **Project Cost-**To be assessed by experts with payback period. Various sectors of economy

especially infrastructure should be given priority to fuel the economy.

4. **Project Plan-** includes but not limited to

    - Budget allocation under various sectors by Planning Commission in line with project cost
    - Work break-down structure
    - Organizing - Critical for getting the project managers work in a synchronized and focused manner

5. **Execution Planning and Implementation-**The most important of all where conflicts among stakeholders derail the project. Here central government should work with state government to get the desired result.

6. **Monitoring -** Catch up plan should be in place with contingencies and risk mitigating strategies.

Leaders should come out of their comfort zone and sit together to examine facts and figures instead of bullying each other's game changing suggestions or solutions. The concept of FDI in retail is the latest fall out of supremacy syndrome without being properly examined, whether the same will FUEL India's success story or not.

In our school days and today also we were asked what you will do when you become Prime Minster of India. Youth parliament is also being conducted at school level to make the students understand how the various bills and law making process is being formulated in a democratic manner. What we are witnessing in today's parliament is unruly scenes which are now affecting the psyche of future generation and they are now further alienating themselves and have reservations for the democratic system of functioning.

Had anybody ever imagined Rabri Devi (not having proper job specification) to be the Chief Minister of Bihar or Rajja Bhaiyya who has been charged with law and order issue is UP jail minister now.

Corruption is now in our blood. We require Dialysis for that, No. So what next, a genuine leadership at the Top with dedicated team members and change of people mindset at large is the only way out to turn-around? There should not be any place for complacency or leniency for corrupted behaviour.

"Sabka bhalla ho aur Sabka sath ho should be the motto". It means we have to carry everybody along on the path of development.

It is high time we should not wait till the hell fall on ourselves. Press the refresh button many times on the India computer screen and remove the junk or spam mail, delete the corrupted files and run the Macfee anti-virus to remove viruses affecting India to get some semblance of hope.

The question today is that we require a pre independence kind of revolution or we require an Egypt kind of revolution or Shri Arvind Kejriwal kind of politics to get people empowered by asking them to give decisions.

The situation in pre Independence era was how to get rid of Britishers or having our own Republic for the people and by the people. Today the situation and problems Indians are facing are multipronged (Reason being systems are not functioning as envisaged by our learned Constitution maker). Today we are fighting our own people to get the systems workable. We also cannot have Egypt like situation where mass movements although turned the table for Hosni

Mubabrak's one man regime, but it had made the country directionless as people are not able to figure out any able leader. Here we have capable leaders in abundance due to our intellectual power but we never learned to work as a team and self-centric orientation overshadowed India. Next comes Arvind Kejriwal brand of politics, which is also not feasible as the common man of this country are engrossed in their daily life not for succeeding in their life but survival is their motto and asking for decisions to arrive at logical conclusion of a problem is too much for them.

Reforms are the key here not only in major constitutional bodies but also required of people and media at mindset level.

Election reforms will set the ball rolling

If and buts should not be part of strict guidelines on the selection of candidates (Job description with minimum qualification for candidate has to be ensured) and also the specific charges against which they can be barred. Candidates have to declare while filing nominations that they have no such charges against them sub-judicial, if there one any charge is, they should get it cleared within a time frame on prima facie basis by court, so that his/her name should be cleared before filing nominations. May be it will create heart burns but no short cut measures. Election should only allow party participation based on regional and national parties status categorically for Lok Sabha or Assembly elections. The evaluation of candidates will not only help in getting some sort of right candidate but also enable younger generation, at least to have looked into the politics seriously as a career or it may encourage people who have settled or performers in life to look it as an option to leverage their success to lessen the suffering of the common man.

The dance of democracy today has somewhat become a mockery of democracy if we continue to elect people on party lines instead of looking at candidates profile also, will continue to widen the gap with China. The exercise of My Vote Counts will then be effective and appreciable.

Judicial and Police Reforms is the next in the offing

Every citizen should be equal and once again repeat, should be equal in the eyes of law. Nobody should be given any preferential treatment. Maximum two appeals at any court should be entitled against the judgment to close the cases. Incentives and reward will galvanize the police work force but also inaction should be seen as non-performance. Improve their working conditions and give them freedom to act without influence as they are already hard pressed. Police force should be educated that their actions should speak that they care for the common people to restore their confidence rather slogan written on their vehicle.

Parliamentary System or Constitutional Reforms

Right to reject or right to recall as propounded by some activists will not serve much purpose as elections are additional expenses and country cannot afford such luxury. What is required is accountability and real measurable commitment from them? The idea here is to make the candidates perform as a full time job. Rajya Sabha, the Upper House should have more people nominated who are experts and can help in formulating policies in their respective fields. Constitutional reforms or amendments should be in the larger interest of the public not for making the problems more grave. Constitutional body like Jan Lokpal should be looked from the perspective of sincere working people who take judicious or risk taking decisions in the interest of the country. What is required is empowerment of officers for taking decisions in the interest of Public as shown by E Sreedharan who had the courage and conviction and did not pay heed to any pressure which may lead to the derailment of the Project. Nobody on earth will take you head-on if you have high integrity, moral and unselfish motives. CBI is acting as *guptchars* to keep the Government informed about the prevailing situations and how much independence should be given to them has become a debatable issue nowadays. Making more laws, more constitutional bodies will increase complexity rather we should strive for the implementation part.

Public Sector Reforms

Perform or perish is the only way out. The Public sectors has lost relevance due to too-much bureaucratic set-up at the top. Give them financial freedom as happened in DMRC to compete with private players. Allow privatization of sick public sectors and also limited privatization for good performers to make them more efficient and market friendly.

Foreign Policy Reforms

As we are in a globalized world, we are affected by various things happening in the world today which affect our economic situations like Indian Currency downslide reflects Indian gloomy economic scenario. We have to carefully choose our partners and allies. Make USA our natural ally in post-cold war era, as many Indians are getting a firm foothold there to leverage our business interests. Try to have a balanced view of the world situation rather taking any extremes to avoid any backlash.

Financial Sector Reforms

We often encounter the share market news going bullish and bearish. This is a speculative market dominated by shares of big players and others in collaboration with stock brokers. The major chunk of profit earning is from share for these big players. They rake mullahs when their shares are up. The Sensex provides a glimpse of the Indian economic situation. Confidence boosting measures are required to get out of current slowdown includes evaluation of MNC proposals for retail sector or other infrastructure projects if it can help beat inflation. Make their business interests aligned to our growth and development interests to have a win-win situation if required skewed more towards India, is a good Idea. India needs change in work-culture which these companies have build over the years and can easily leverage the same on a risk sharing basis.

Today the main concerns for the common people or middle class are inflation and housing. Tax re-structure and Housing loan rates should be the main focus. Half the cost in the prices of diesel and petrol is from the state levied taxes. States should look for other avenues for their income like setting up more SEZ's and commissioning for their capital expenditure to get payback to get relief to the common man. The money allocated by Planning Commission to various states should be accounted for and every state government should publish their balance-sheet. RBI should encourage the banking sector by revising CRR (Credit Reserve Ratio) ratio and check the money circulation to boost the realty sector.

Reforms of People mindset

Oprah Winfrey a famous TV anchor of USA , when she came to India, in one of her interviews said, "traffic signals are like dancing lights in India as everybody jumping over it." The best way to enforce the culture of discipline is to start implementing the traffic rules in full swing without any bias or favour; you will find the same will immediately have a positive impact on the people mindset. People started wearing safety belts in the car once Supreme Court has given the strict rulings. Look at Singapore (one of the smallest countries with mixed breed of culture ranging from Chinese to Indian settlers) despite limited resources is one of the best economies of the world and the financial hub of the Asia-Pacific region. The basic reason for their success is hard work, discipline, law abiding and no non-sense attitude of their citizens and also law enforcement agencies have given full authority to do with any hooligans. We are not self-starters; we are forced to work, play the game of passing the pass and inclined to break laws given a chance. The example of MGNAREGA (Mahatma Gandhi National Rural Employment Guarantee Act), a very good scheme of Government requires review as rural people are now getting easy money through these schemes without doing serious physical work for which they are employed. Some public servants today work, thinking that they are doing some kind of a charity for the country. Actually they are slowly cutting the tree which has given those fruits for several years and still then no sign of learning. We are today RIDING on a slow sinking TITANIC, unless some drastic measures are taken. People have herd mentality, so riding on this fact, only way to implement and change mindsets is to have deterrents like fine in place for not obeying rules and regulations with strict instruction for enforcing agencies to implement the same without any side dealings. Any officer found napping should be taken to task. Incentives should be given to farmers for more productivity to foster work culture at rural level. Their children should be employed under the various schemes by proving proper education and skill development trainings. Industrialists should be encouraged for setting of plants with SEZ kind of concepts in those areas to help the local people employed. At town or urban level, create various Singapores within India instead of creating more states.

People should come out of their shell from caste or creed politics and appeal to the parties to get responsible and accountable, candidates with clean image should be selected or projected. People who can really devote time to their constituency should be given the ticket.

Please remember, India is caught in a vicious cycle of uncertainty and instability and getting a stable and accountable Government in place is the key for critical success factor for India. We have already had such scenario in the late 90s and early 2000 during which our all-round growth had taken some beating where we had several prime ministers and several prime ministers in waiting. People knowingly or unknowingly voting on party or caste lines take pride when their supported candidate wins, but ultimately in the long run we and our young generations become the victims or sufferer of our selfish judgments.

Younger generation is the key today who are active on social media but not trading the ground realities. Mall, Music, Pizza, Parties, Laptop, Facebook, What's App, other social gatherings are their favourite pastime as they have already turned a blind eye to the prevailing situations. Education system is not skill oriented although we are churning large number of Graduates/Engineers/MBAs. Younger generation dream of big time quick money but where are the jobs except for the IT Industry. Today the young generation is smart and capable of taking decisions but directionless. It is our duty to see that this Maggie generation abundance energy is being channelized for their self-sustenance and re-orient them towards India. Young mind should know that financial burden with which middle class family suffers. They should help their parents by becoming at least good children. Stop free money to them as it is worth nil than hard earned money. Encourage industries to generate jobs by giving them leewayds and may consider increasing the FDI CAP in infrastructure. Reward the talent with higher positions in Government jobs and have real competition for such posts. Lastly, keep politics out of such positions to have credibility in the eyes of Fuchchas (as younger generation refer themselves in the colleges). It is like having Nav-Ratnas (experts who can take important policy decisions with bureaucrats acting as facilitators) in the armory of the Government, as Akbar had in his courtyard. We care for you should be the Government motto.

A famous book says "You can win but you will never win unless you change your mindset".

Reforms of Media Mindset

Today India is limited to New Delhi only thanks to our TV media. Whatever happens in Delhi especially news on political happenings which are somewhat non-existence in the mind of today's younger generation are being reported 24 hours with new raga every day and leaving many questions unanswered in the mind of people to debate among themselves, brownie points being scored by debater's and mad rush for TRPs resulted in the real issues being lost. News break on the same day and dies the next day. Media latch on to the next juggernaut and no follow-up being made. The Nirbhaya case has been dealt in media rightly for long and it not only sensitizes the people but also resulted in formulation of law for such cases, but has the ground reality changed? Political jugalbandi (Instruments played in synchronized but making different sounds) is being played everyday. It is said that when Rome was burning, Nero was playing instrument. Today, the scenario is same - India is lost while the instrument is continued to be played on TV channels. Praise and get on board our real unsung heroes and experts in their respective fields and make their views also count for fruitful discussions.

What media requires, being the most visible and acceptable mode and being perception builders, is to highlight the plight of common man and try to force the issue, by getting leaders committed for the development without any false promises and see the next time they are invited, they should come full of goodies rather doing a NaMo, Raga, Muffler praising all the time.

Media has done a great job in supporting Anna Movement against corruption to the fullest without any flip flops which had attracted people right from the children to the older generation alike and this success is the winner all the way.

Media in newspapers sometimes also publish some news and articles which are skewed. I will just quote one article which I have read in the recent past before elections, which says why NaMo was scoring over Raga and Muffler, the question here is not who is scoring what, what India will get by electing people, as if populist measures or promises made in manifestoes or speeches will do wonders and will turn it around for India without having any concrete road map. The situation today is very demanding and challenging, we have to ask tough questions regarding vision and mission of parties rather simply toeing their lines. The best example of such anomaly is Ms. Mamta Banerjee and Shri Arvind Kejriwal, they have all the good intentions for the common or poor people but when they faced the Moment of truth or harsh reality, failed to take-off initially as they did not have any road map to implement their ideas or having experts in their kitty to get the job done. We have one recent ad going around "No wuloo banoing"(Means we should not be taken for granted).

Media should remember their responsibility is paramount in today's world, running after TRP will help you in the short run but India will be left behind in Delhi's syndrome. Impartial and Proactive Media will make a huge difference for this country.

If we today fail in our duty, our future generations and freedom fighters will always reprimand us and it is our duty to see formation of a stable Government, preserve our democratic set up by electing people who can make difference in India's fortune rather their fortunes. An economically sound country is the real success rather having so many prime ministerial candidates in waiting.

I appeal to the younger generations including myself (I also feel I am younger but with some experience now), fellow countrymen to be the torch bearer and try to become game changer for this great country before it is too late to make our presence felt rather than solving the problems faced by the country on social media. Remember, today our systems are such they will make you believe that from a filled glass, you deserve only half or less filled glass and rest half or more of the glass is theirs.

Greatness vs Great

"Greatness is like payback time to the stakeholders rather becoming money mongers or more back channel rewards?"

You have often heard people saying what a great guy and girl he or she is? Does it mean they are champions in a particular field or champions of champion in every aspect of life? Greatness is the later stage. People become great in their respective fields but fail to achieve greatness. Whereas people who are ordinary at first instance make the cut. Mahatma Gandhi is the classic example of Greatness. He had not graduated from Harvard School, he rather understood the Human Touch theory. The problem begins when great people start getting GOD like status. Greatness eluded some of the great personalities of our time like Tiger Woods, Mike Tyson, Michael Jackson, Bill Clinton, Maradona, not because they are not talented but they have alienated themselves from people by their behaviour. Greatness is like going NEARER to GOD, to have more politeness in the core of the soul but not being called GOD. Striving for more power for selfish gains is the root cause for such failures and mismatch between what is portrayed and what is behind the scenes executed by such personalities. What is required to understand after all you are Human and you may not be the last man standing when everything is finished in this world. Look at Chinese sports player in the Olympics, away from media attention, methodical in their approach, great calm the hallmark and nimble feet and satisfaction personified after their routine, not bothered about the result is what is called greatness, unlike our sporting heroes. Greed and Ego has become the hallmark of some of the celebrated and media perpetuated personalities. Gracious in defeat is also the hallmark of greatness as happened to Usain bolt after he got defeated. The resolve to bounce back and respect for rivals is the sign of character. We are normally swayed away by media frenzy without getting the facts verified. TV Media today is the famous pide piper of Hamlin. In India, Sachin has been one of the most celebrated personalities while the claim of some others greats being ignored. Sachin the "Bharat Ratna" had enthralled the Indian people with his batting prowess for the past 20 years. Statistics were his baby. Great Sir Don Bradman had once bestowed his blessings. Being darling of Masses, Media and Corporate house is all sign of greatness.

Greatness is not something which can be given on a platter to anybody as it requires critical examination. Greatness shall be bestowed on persons especially based on their behavioral aspects and how they take the people along their path of glory. Sachin represents the Indian mentality of being an individual greater than the team. India loses or wins, Sachin was always first because of his sheer talent and performance. Sachin's real glory years were between 1996-2000 when he was ruling the roost and he was humble along with the fame. But team India was on receiving end during these years. Team India's success revolves around Sachins success and it was not performing as a unit. The main reason was Sachin persona had taken over the psyche of Indian cricketers with the slogan being played everywhere—Sachin out, India out. When he was on the peak, team India was never a force to reckon with especially in test cricket, their performance abroad was abysmal. The situation changed after 2000 and India reached the pinnacle of test cricket ruled once by Australians and crowned No.1 when they performed as a unit. Sachin occupied his position somewhat longer despite his inconsistent performance during the fag end of his career as his reflexes were not on his side whereas people around him like Mark, Steve, Mathew Hayden, Gilchrist, Macgrath retired despite of more cricketing years ahead of them. He got the support from BCCI controlled administrators/commentators and some media rather from his one-time committed supporters in masses. The manner in which he achieved his 100th century against Bangladesh which India lost and the way he prolonged his career was being seen through the lenses. We should be open to constructive criticism and consider it as a part and parcel of life to move ahead. The money mongers of this world created a win-lose situation to get maximum mileage out of his brand during the end of his cricketing career rather helping him in achieving greatness in his final days. It was bad and unbecoming on the part of some media who instead of highlighting the performance of other players responsible for the Indian Victory, instead put front page news on him regarding his dismissal or on some of his antics. Such people like Sachin have the love of masses which is a rarity in life and bestowed on few chosen one by God once in a century who lift the morale of already hard pressed people by their divine talent, are beyond any award and reward. Here the point is not taking anything away from stupendous achievements of Greats like Sachin, but to make people understand that even if they are not champions in their field but they can make a difference in the life by spreading smile all around without any expectation of being rewarded. Mother Teresa is the epitome of such greatness.

Core of greatness is the pleasure of giving and Greatness is well said in the following lines from the famous Hindi poem

पुष्प की अभिलाषा

चाह नहीं मैं सुरबाला के
गहनों में गूंथा जाऊँ

चाह नहीं, प्रेमी-माला में
बिंध प्यारी को ललचाऊँ

चाह नहीं, सम्राटों के शव
पर हे हरि, डाला जाऊँ

चाह नहीं, देवों के सिर पर
चढ़ूँ भाग्य पर इठलाऊँ

मुझे तोड़ लेना वनमाली
उस पथ पर देना तुम फेंक

मातृभूमि पर शीश चढ़ाने
जिस पर जावें वीर अनेक।।

English Translation

Title : Wish of a Flower

Line - 1 : Flower does not wish to get stuck in the ornaments made out of it.

Line - 2 : Flower does not wish to get stuck in the hair of a lover.

Line-3 : Flower does not wish to get flowered on the dead bodies of kings and queens or powerful persons.

Line -4 : Flower does not wish to get stuck in the hair of a lover .

Line - 5 : Flower does not wish to get stuck in the head of an angel.

Line-6: Flower wants the gardener to pluck him and throw it on the path of brave people who defend and laid their lives for the sake of country.

The basic funda of the above lines is Greatness is like payback time to the stakeholders rather becoming money mongers or more back channel rewards before bidding adieu to the world. Greatness is how you remain cool, calm and collected, when the chips are down and people are baying for your blood.

Look at Bill Gates, the world's richest man, down to earth, changed human lives with technological advances is now busy working for human race survival.

The gap between the super-rich Indians and the poor man is exponentially increasing day by day and also India's fiscal deficit is widening day by day as compared to their supernormal profit.

Everybody whether it is an individual or a company has the right to maximize its wealth but at what cost. Today family values are fast degenerating and societal status is determined by Money and Money only. I will quote the famous quote of Late Judeo Singh, MP from Chhatisgarh in this regard as under:-

"Paisa to khuda nahi, par khuda ki kasam
Khuda se kamm bhi nahi"

(if money is not GOD, but it is no less than GOD).

Please ask yourself a simple question "How much money you require" knowing that you will not be there to enjoy and you require only two chapattis to eat that too in peace. Money also brings curse along with materialistic happiness. Another curious case of Ponty Chadha, Liquor Baron of NCR was the causality of such curse which resulted in loss of near and dear ones. Money will not buy you longevity as happened in the case of Shri Dhiru Bhai Ambani (Founder of Reliance Industries) but it definitely prolonged the inevitable.

There is one old saying *"Bhagwan ki lathi mein awaz nahi hoti"* (Means GOD makes their presence felt without making sound). What goes around comes around.

I will narrate one simple story written by the famous writer Leo Tolstoy which I had read in Hindi version from my daughter class 6th book to peep into the level human greed can go.

A farmer was on a buying spree of a remote land sale for few rupees as today's builders are doing and selling them at higher price afterwards and became superrich.

The farmer met Bhils Sardar (King) in the process, who placed a condition that he would sell all the measured land for a mere 10000 rupees only, if he managed to cover and measure the distance on his foot and come back at the starting point in the evening before the sunset. The farmer started and as he moved he wanted to maximize the measurement till the sunset. Soon he was so engrossed he did not even take food and lunch during his journey. Suddenly he realized, he was very tired, and time was too short to get back to the starting point. The greed for more left him with dire consequences; he fell down and died due to hunger. He was finally buried in the 5 feet dug out in the land. People or Bhils Sardar (King) sarcastically remarked *"Bas akhir itni jameen"* (Means you require only 5 feet dug out when you die, so do not chant for more-more).

I will just quote an old saying in one of the Indian Dialect

"Hum churiye nerreye nerreye, Khuda Churaye eke bariye". It simply means we work hard through our life for money, assets, fame by bullying people, subordinates, peers getting heart burns in return but it is the act of GOD at some stage of life which makes all the difference and restores parity. You have to pay for your sins in this world only. The only problem here is that GOD takes time in giving justice but he gives you all the time in this world, at least to correct some of your wrong doings. But we never learn and commit the same mistakes again and again. There is one famous story in Mahabharata, there was one character called Shishupal who had been given immunity by Lord Krishna that he could abuse him 100 times afterwards his immunity expired. In one of the meeting, he kept on abusing Lord Krishna and Lord Krishna kept on reminding him and counting the abuses in front of him. Shishupal continued his abusing spree despite warning and got his head removed by Sudharshan Chakra carried by Lord Krishna once the 100 abuses were over.

Please note that of all the Mughal Emperors, only Akbar is being remembered for his Human Touch theory, not for his wealth or land he acquired.

I will just share one simple and famous story of a great human being with great heart about Sir Abraham Lincoln, the first President of America. According to the story, Lincoln was riding with a friend in a carriage on a rainy evening. As they rode, Lincoln told the friend that he believed in what economists would call the utility-maximizing theory of behavior, that people always act so as to maximize their own happiness, and for no other reason. Just then, the carriage crossed a bridge, and Lincoln saw a pig stuck in the muddy riverbank. Telling the carriage driver to stop, Lincoln struggled through the rain and mud, picked up the pig, and carried it to safety. When the muddy Lincoln returned to the carriage, his friend naturally pointed out that he had just disproved his own hypothesis by putting himself to great trouble and discomfort to save a pig. "Not at all," said Lincoln. "What I did is perfectly consistent with my theory. If I hadn't saved that pig, I would have felt terrible. Just like a step on the moon is a giant step for mankind, Sir Lincoln had taken a giant leap to reach the height of greatness. We have to work hard for the removal of hurdles from the path of common people and leverage our greatness to make the life easier for them.

We request all the Ambanis, Tatas, Birlas and other industrialists who over the years has done good for themselves and also for India, but for achieving greatness, please work for India's excellence.

Part-3

Conclusion

"Who will have the last laugh or whose winning is always a success?"

So finally who will have the last laugh or whose winning is always a success?

Only GOD has the last laugh, You will die some day, so die with a big heart to have a lasting positive impression on people and make your winning always a success.

Try to become once again 2-3 years old child who has no inhibitions, flows like a river, and gives you the joy without any prejudice or bias with his little efforts and stammering voice to reinvent yourself.

Try to walk an extra mile for yourself and for others as well. The only persons who claim to be successful the ones having fewer enemies and more admirers. Winning is not always a symbol of success, your success rate depends on how many persons you have positive impact in your life. Realization of being left stranded only comes when people lose their powerful positions and fall out of their own wrong doing as they created more enemies by their authoritative behaviour. It is said in the following lines (Hindi Version)

" Yey jaroori nahi, ki mera naam har pathar aur mehloon pe khuda ho, jaroori yey hai ki mera naam har dil pe khuda ho".

It means it is only important to have your name engraved on the hearts of people not on the stones meant for inaugurations.

Nobody will give you the power, you have to exercise power in a dignified manner. Never run away from a problem, confront it. Otherwise having an ostrich like syndrome will ruin your life. Remember every cloud has a silver lining. If you have clear vision, you will definitely have clear plans to achieve. Remember, the following lines (Hindi Version)

"Kabhi Kissie ko Mukkamal Jahan nahi milta",
Kabhi jameen to Kabhi asmann nahi milta"

It means you will never find peace in life if you are searching the best of both worlds. Every dog has its day but the perseverance and patience is what makes the difference between a real winner and dog.

Follow your passion (like playing guitar, screaming at lonely place, driving a bike on the mountains or whatever you feel like doing) which might have been denied many times due to important priorities in life and remove all inhibitions (when you have no inhibition you perform better) for some time of your journey in life to ensure that you are not a mechanical robot but alive and kicking. Be original and cherish your originality. Please take care of yourself for your own survival and do soul searching from time to time.

Please remember—the famous title of the movie "Zindagi nahi mileage dobara"- Means you will not get a second life for resurrecting your life as per your liking.

Watch movies like "Tare Jammeen Par", "Munna Bhai MBBS," "Three idiots" or any other inspirational movies to come to terms with the nuances of human life. Do a Funkshuk Wangroo of three idiots every now and then. Do a GAP analysis to know what others require about you or where you are lagging in terms of performance metrics or critical success factors. Create "WOW" Moments and more win-win situations in life.

There is one famous saying "Success has many fathers but failure has no takers". But today, the same saying is somewhat reversed, failure has many takers but success has selfish fathers to take maximum out of it, till you put the wrong foot forward. People enjoy talking about failures and try to belittle your success. It is very difficult to remain good in life. People today have very short memory. Nobody remembers once you are gone. Make surroundings conducive for everyone even for a child to flourish. The only thing you can do is "Enjoy the life and let others also enjoy, bring smiles to other faces, you will definitely die in peace knowing that you are successful."

"Khudi ko kar buland itna, ki har taqdeer se pehley, Khuda khud bandey se poochey bol teri raza kya hai"

It means you should have your self-esteem, integrity , honesty not ego to the highest order, GOD will definitely ask you first for your wishes before granting to anybody else.

We as a society are fast becoming Dhritarastras (The king of Hastinapur who was blind and remained blind or allowed continuance of evil desires of his son Duryodhan in the epic Hindu mythology *Mahabharata*) and leg pullers, rather appreciating the efforts of good people around. The country will only succeed if at micro or society level we build trust, spread happiness, make our children responsible for taking the baton to achieve new heights. The festival celebration is the time to build more trust. For a healthy society we have to inculcate culture of critical reasoning not have preconceived notions. The examination conducted by GMAT for MBA admission all around the world is primarily based on this concept. Analyzing the situation and coming out of logical decisions is the hall mark of many developed countries. We as a society are followers of our masters. The "why why" or root cause analysis are some of the management concept to get the things in the right perspective. We should respect each other's viewpoints and mannerism, considering the background and environment we have been brought up rather ridiculing or brushing aside just to show superiority. All are not well equipped for the discussion and to get our point across or have consensus, logical conclusion with facts and figures is the way out. We all are talented bunch of people, the recipe for our success or challenge is to make it an appreciating society.

India is lying low today. The idea of "United We Stand" is more relevant today than in the past, considering the fact that some time back China's official newspaper published an article stating that India was a fragmented society and it could crumble at any time. While India is besieged and is on the back foot by internal bickering and unresolved issues with hostile neighbours, China has fast become the breeding ground for performers. Indian people and our leaders mindset require a sea change to begin with and make ourselves a force to reckon-with by performing. Our neighbouring countries are fighting for *Thodi si jameen and Thoda sa aasmann* (Means fighting for more space). Instead of making such issues as point of inflexion or creation of more failed states, common people of the region only want peace, better education and living for their children. We are all brothers and sisters; forget past animosity as it only helps others to thrive on our wounds. We have to work together in the interest of our people's well-being. Hysteria of creating war like situations laden with weapons of mass destruction will lead us nowhere. Future of world lies in the Indian region only. Success of talented people of this region will be the real game changer provided leaderships should look beyond petty politics. Human lives and generations lost is what we will be finally achieving. The increase in the amount of spending for defense is all non-productive assets; we are getting year after year. Prevail upon the hardliners for the success of the region. Winning wars and leaving scars on the minds of the people is not success. Please note that it is our own country which has been secured after 100 years of freedom struggle and blood of our beloved freedom fighters. We should make their success count.

So finally what are the success metrics for winning always?

It is hard to define but in simple terms we can at least draw some kind of matrix to get a feel of it.

Home Success (Getting the family succeed) (II)	**Professional Success** (Getting the team and company succeed) (I)
Personal Success (Getting the learning succeed) (III)	**Behavioural Success** (Getting the society, and company succeed at large) (IV)

Analysis of matrix

If you see the left part (Quadrant II + III) of success matrix, you will find it is more of a situation you can change or it is in your domain, while the right part (Quadrant I + IV) of your success is more driven by others. More winning towards right side (Quadrant I + IV) of matrix will lead you towards greatness. More winning towards left side (Quadrant II + III) of the matrix will make your success a true winner. Right diagonal success (Quadrant I + III) is your personal acumen. Left diagonal success (Quadrant II + IV) is your personal relationship. The Success in quadrant II+IV will foster a culture of values system (Honesty, Integrity, Care, Trust, Respect, Accountability, Responsibility, Country/ Family first) which is fast degenerating in our society. The success in quadrant I+III will foster culture of self-respect , passion to succeed, refinement of thought, critical reasoning, down to earth attitude, stress–free environment, work-home balance, team-work, problem solving culture, less conflicts, more innovation, out of the box thinking, thinking beyond Z will improve bottom line includes people. Behavioural success is like icing on the cake. Since today the world is marred by situational complexities and quick and risk mitigating decisions, making a balancing act is like walking on a tight rope having dead ends. Remember complete slip-up on any front will cause irreparable damage and will have a cascading effect on other fronts in future and also for future generations. The best you can do is to minimize heart burns while climbing up the ladder.

Please also remember till now only Mother Earth is the planet known where GOD has been kind enough to have all the ingredients for the success of human race. Do not belittle the effort of GOD by our own foolish effort destroying the world in the mad rush for power and supremacy ignoring the wishes of Mother Nature. We should now stand-up and salute all those human beings who have made our life beautiful and help in the growth of human civilization in whatever capacity and helping the Mother Nature for the survival of the human race. They are our real winners and unsung heroes worth emulating them.

Part-4

Lessons learnt from the Elections

"Amazing Election or Amazing NaMo."

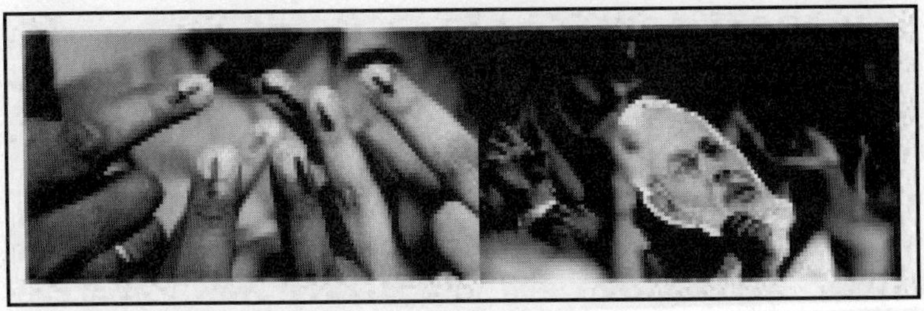

"Amazing Election or Amazing NaMo."

While I was writing the last chapter of my book, New Popular Government just came in place at New Delhi.

Amazing Election

This election result has brought new thinking and new possibilities for India. The crux of the results is the people maturity and young people desperation to redeem themselves for development only and people deserve standing ovation for finally coming out of caste, creed, religion politics to have a stable Government at the Centre.

In my introduction and preface, I have pointed out the complacency syndrome which is the root cause of downfall of person or organization. I will not analyze the things as many expert will see this result, but in manner to highlight the essence of this book to give the reader better insight.

The UPA-II government started on promising note with Indian GDP being talked about internationally and future of Indian economy looking north (Feel good factors were in place).

During 2010-2011, the subprime crisis leading to economic slowdown in the USA and continuous increase in the crude prices had cascading effect on the economy of India and which had finally resulted in decline in GDP on continuous basis. The Commonwealth Game mismanagement had further dented India's Image world-wide and the market sentiments suddenly nose-dived. The euphoria of being compared with China on growth front had taken backseat. The lack of control on various ministries as reported in the media had further compounded the problem. The delay in taking quid-pro quo actions on various issues (Like Inflation and various reported scams in media) and handling the Anna Movement on corruption (which was the major issue playing in the minds of Indians at that time) had dented the image of UPA-II. The culmination of all such events had finally resulted in their defeat. Despite of having best of experienced Project managers to deliver the Goods, the complacency syndrome (We are the best and We can do no wrong) might have caught up with UPA-II.

The election bigul started in 2012 itself and formation of AAM Admi Party in that year, signaled the things to happen in coming months.

Prelude of this election brings various facets of Indian Polity (Change of political enemies at various point in time) , UPA-II was the target of rest including media with AAM Admi Party became the toast of the nation, after AAM Admi Party hara-kiri in Delhi they become the target of rest and on the election eve NDA led by Prime Minister Narendra Modi, with proven track record of delivering prosperity in Gujarat became the toast of the nation and finally delivered the knock-out punch.

This election is a case of tale of two Chief Ministers - Arvind Kejriwal and Shri Narendra Modi. The fall out of previous Government was mainly attributable to the rotten system which has finally yielded for non-performance.

Shri Arvind Kejriwal with all the hard skills (Best of education) was given the mandate in New Delhi, may have lacked administrative skills or some soft skills as a result of being inexperienced. Some of the decisions taken by his Government defy all the logic and the end result being sidelined for the present.

Our new Prime Minister, Narendra Modi, had achieved something great what the predecessors failed to achieve in the recent past, getting absolute majority riding on developmental planks. He might lack in some hard skills but his administrative and man management skill was the highlight of this election. We all hope whatever his Gujarat Model as talked about, he will have an INDIA First Model to get India going as alive and kicking and will organize team, formalize a concrete road map and deliverables to do it.

"Amazing NaMo"

The amazing election campaign carried by Narendra

Modi covering across the length and breadth of the country tirelessly and non-stop, reminds me of new movie the `Amazing Spiderman'. Although he led the election but the importance of team work (Main thrust of this book) was the hall mark of his successful campaign. He also acknowledged the effort of backstage workers.

His projection as PM candidate much earlier was a masterstroke and gave him the first mover advantage to lead the mission 272. He is a leader who sees an opportunity and takes faster decision as per the merit of the case. Unlike many CM's who continued to think or delayed their decisions, he immediately provided TATA scrapped Nano project, a new lease of life in Gujarat. A good leader always thinks beyond Z. He redefined the whole concept of marketing a brand and taken it to a new level which appealed to the people in this election. The concept of brand will only be successful if the Brand has substance or credibility. Each member of his team was well aware of his role and responsibility. Everybody was aligned to the same objective of getting 272. Once you are synchronized and focused, success bound to happen. Market segmentation as called in marketing was amply demonstrated by focusing on UP and Bihar as key states which finally helped them to achieve the unthinkable. Brand reinforcement done by carrying out *Chai pe charcha* like initiatives to connect with the people. Tagged line like *"Achey Din Anney wale hain"* had clicked with the voters. Finally word of mouth - His credibility to deliver the prosperity was carried by migrant workers in Gujarat to their respective states as one news article put it, made all the difference.

This election will always be remembered for People's resolve for better India and NaMo magic or his team strike rate in getting the magical figure of 300 plus which looked unthinkable even during the initial counting of votes.

Agenda for the New Government

"Restoring Exiled India in BRIC"

Several writers, analysts, experts and critics will once again set the agenda for the New Government and will question each move of the Government and want turnaround in a few months. Previous Government had claimed to curtail the Inflation within 100 days and same did not happen, as economy today is being driven by various factors in the globalized market place which are beyond Government control. We should not be judgmental in our approach rather analytical and wait for the road map in terms of measurable performance metrics to deliver within a certain time frame. (Settling time period is the key for the new Government—How fast they will act).The time gap between settling time and taking action will be the critical success factor for this Government as people are impatient to see the results.

Please remember, the success of South East Asian Countries like South Korea, Japan was fuelled by their reform policies and hard work culture but their subsequent decline in growth rate is because, they failed to insulate themselves from the market dynamics of demand and supply and exchange rate fluctuations. When you do not have demand or people not willing to pay for your product, idling inventory will lead to recession. China, the so called new King of the world economy has demonstrated what it takes to have their GDP (Gross Domestic Product) on ascendency on consistent basis and it did not happen overnight. Proper planning and its execution on time bound manner is the key success factor. Each town/villages has become a business/manufacturing unit and the population which was a bottleneck for them, has suddenly become the driving force of their economy. The goods produced with cheap labour cost and with improved infrastructure resulted in high volume production with incomparable low prices being sold throughout the world (Volume Based Success Story).

India today is not talked about in the same breath as other fast growing economies—BRIC. The reason being that economic reforms are not backed by the checks and balances. Unlike China, we are importing much more than exporting, as the cost of production is higher in India despite cheap labour cost. Ad-hochism in our system brings inefficiencies and delay the decision making process. The various infrastructure projects are needed to reduce cost of production for which funds are required.

OPPORTUNITIES have been given to many people in the past. Have they delivered what was required from them?

The new Government has the requisite and decisive mandate to fire all cylinders.

So what will be their Agenda or menu on their platter?

Various suggestions already mentioned in the book for the minimum required. In a nutshell, our economic policies may require immediate review in line with new global scenario and economic meltdown, identification and consolidation of sectors which can fuel economy and arrangement of funds to fund the capital expenditure.

From the Author's point of view, if we do four simple things immediately (although tough to achieve in present circumstances, but not impossible), we will definitely set the ball rolling.

1. Try to simplify the governmental procedures and guidelines to foster faster decision making process.

2. Focus on fewer or critical tasks initially (like reviving sagging economy to provide breather for the common man) and avoid opening too many fronts.

3. Make people accountable who are facing the moment of truth and empowered them for judicious decisions

4. Take the help of experts but do not over do it (too many cooks) and get the gut feeling going to take the project "Bharat Vijai Bhavo" a reality.

In a democratic set up, getting consensus for bold decisions require great deal of Leadership maturity.

The new Government has to guard against the complacency and work with an open mind rather focusing on non-issues which are not productive but counter productive. Plan with execution strategy and have project managers who can deliver and should be the part of the team and set review mechanisms to have the earlier payback period for the benefits of the common man of this country.

MOTTO SHOULD BE "JUST DO IT" AS WE DO NOT HAVE TIME TO PONDER

If China can achieve the success with a single minded approach to get better of their western counterpart, Why not India having the best Intellectual property in their basket. No matter what, we have to agree (not agree to disagree and opposing for the sake of opposition) if India has to win freedom against corruption, inflation, poverty, economic slumber or else we have to remain exiled from BRIC.

Taming Inflation

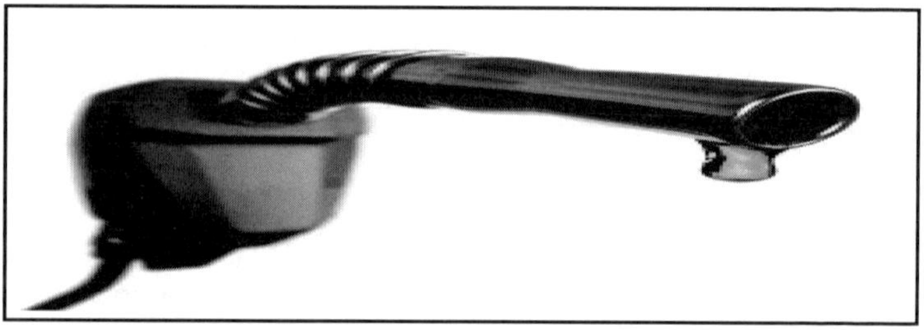

"Is it really possible to reduce the prices of petrol and diesel ?" An Achilles heel for the Government requires Critical Analysis.

The very fact that the fixation of petroleum prices especially for petrol and diesel is based on Product Parity Price calculated on the basis of import and export parity (in simple terms what price we have to pay if we import and export the product), the reduction mechanism has to be looked from various angles. The refiners are already running on thin wafer margins due to increase in Crude prices over 100 USD/barrel. The so called oil pool deficit due to subsidy provided on Product Parity Price is increasing day by day. The government has to do a fine balancing act and has to walk on tight rope to pass the best possible prices to consumer considering the prevailing market scenario. Taxes levied by government constitute around 35-40% of the final product price which is the major source for revenue for them. Dollar exchange rate fluctuations on higher side also vitiated the already charged pricing environment. Unprecedented rise in prices of petroleum products require some innovative short term measures as prices are in tandem with market dynamics.

But the basic question remains: Can we reduce the prices considering the above facts?

Bottom line of Refinery reflects as under:

Gross Refining margin (GRM) = Product Sale at Parity Price* – Cost of production

*Excludes Subsidies, taxes, profit or other cost added to give final price to the customer

The benefit to consumer in terms of pricing and better profit margins for refiners to sustain their operations in light of high crude prices, can either be achieved by lowering cost of production or having a better pricing mechanism to create a win-win situation. We have to identify the petroleum sector as the most important strategic sector unlike other PSUs and rules and regulations should be made more flexible for their working and strategic decision making.

Two pronged strategy will help us in taming the prices by adding up incremental margins at various stages of processing right from supply of inputs to Output available to customer (The whole gamete or chain has to be analysed)

1. **The cost identification approach:** We have to identify the controllable and uncontrollable cost factors at first level.

2. **The procedural approach:** We have to identify the flaws if any in present mechanism in the entire supply-chain to have best suited cost-effective mechanism. This is based on the notion that system inefficiencies or delay in systems and its non-optimization only adds to cost and leads to opportunity lost.

Now I will explain some areas where we can use the above strategies.

Parameters which have Indirect Impact on pricing

Crude Procurement (Uncontrollable)

Major chunk of the cost involved is in the crude buying - We have two varieties of crude available in the market :

1. High Sulphur Crude (Costing less per Barrel), require additional technology/processing costs to convert into low sulphur to meet the EURO norms product.

2. Low Sulphur Crude (Costing more per Barrel)

Today we are buying both crudes based on its availability in the international market and inventories level at the refineries.

Another uncontrollable cost involved here is freight charges to bring it to the Indian Shore which may be some percentage of crude cost.

Crude Basket mixing and lining of freight forwarder both on long term and short term basis are the two critical success factors which can give us huge incremental advantage. This is a high fluctuating and high risk market, quick decisions with full transparency for buying and selling cargoes based on perceived advantage with risk mitigating strategies in place based on the information available at that point of time will definitely save lot of money rather following certain procedural requirements and guidelines. Such practices may lack the ability of capturing market opportunities like availability of distress cargoes, arbitrage opportunities, flexibilities with respect to cargo sizes, loading dates, co-loading of cargoes, outright sale of cargoes in case of refinery outages etc. Remove infrastructural constraints in loading and unloading of crude at Port which may add up to the costs of bringing to Indian shore. Strategic reserves of crude may be kept instead of keeping three to four months inventories to tackle price fluctuations. If we save money and reduce the buying cost of crude to some extent, we may pass the advantage to consumers.

Another way is to find out New Oil and Gas fields by upstream companies to shelve some of the dependence on importing crude and to have alternate viable low cost of energy.

The upstream oil and gas industry is a key stakeholder in the energy security and climate change debate, and would play a significant role in promoting clean and sustainable energy use all along the entire oil and gas value chain.

As the future of world is energy sector and the future real war will be fought for energy security, long term contracts with potential partners by pooling of resources to leverage benefits on each other will be the order of the day. Countries like India where the demand of energy has increased multi folds will have to go for the kill even if it requires bending much more than required.

The exploration requires huge investments and getting efficient technology in place will require lot of expertise.

"BRIC" may help India especially China and Russia who have close co-operation with countries having oil and gas fields. Expand "BRIC" and include other countries like

Iran, Turkey, who can pool their resources for benefits and business interests of member countries in the same line as other Groups OPEC, ASEAN are operating instead of sitting back as an idle group. If such association happened, then it will be a major achievement for energy security for India. Meanwhile continue to explore other African, Asian and South African countries that may have oil reserves.

The Indian Terrain is also being explored under new NELP (New Exploration and Licensing Policy). We have private players like Reliance, BP, Cairn energy operating along with Government flagship companies ONGC and OIL. It is healthy sign that these companies have find reserves on the Indian Shore and we hope many more findings will happen in the near future. Government has to devise some mechanisms to pass the benefits to Indian users for such activities but also to ensure continuance of such activities. One way is to optimize the pricing by discussing with all the stakeholders considering the future prospects and problems of such capital intensive operations where probability of success is skewed in the negative sides.

Operational Efficiency (Controllable)

The running of plant with close to maximum out put and minimum loss of utilities will lead to effective operation. This will not only help conversion of any idling inventories of crude but also reduce cost of production. Improvement in operational efficiency is a challenge for the refiners and they are working tirelessly on this. Improved GRM may leverage some price advantage for the customers as well.

Parameters which have direct impact on pricing

Product Parity Price (Uncontrollable)

Parikh Committee report along with their recommendations is available on net in this regard based on detailed analysis (http://petroleum.nic.in/parikh.pdf), however, I will be presenting only the take-always for the sake of simplicity and understanding and key areas to be attacked only.

Before going into the analyzing part we have to revisit the current scenario in which we are operating:

The prices based on import/export parity price have merely moved in tandem with the international prices after deregulation. The government could not take the burden for it more than what it already takes in the form of heavy subsidies for various petroleum products. Time is running out for oil companies as their balance sheets are now showing considerable decrease in profit margins. The oil companies require considerable amount of funds for their capital investments for their expansion and upgradation projects to meet the growing demand. They cannot be simply dependent on the return by price hike as it only helps them to bear the operational expenditure and repayment of huge borrowings made for capital investments. The government is now facing a Catch 22 situation. It knows that if it does nothing, these companies will become unviable. But if it raises oil prices, it might invite a voter backlash. A trade-off between Good economics and Good politics is required. It is the time everybody has to face this harsh reality.

This debate should, therefore, be reframed. It should not be about whether prices should be raised or not, to give relief to particularly the poor people who are reeling under heavy pressure of inflation. It should also be about the steps required to pull the companies back from the brink of financial collapse.

Is it really possible to have some mechanism to control the product parity price at refinery level in such a way to insulate the consumers and help the oil companies from the loss due to under recoveries?

We have to first look at the product parity pricing (PPP). The only thing here which can be controlled may be custom duty levied to reach the PPP price OR there could be any better way to operate such pricing mechanism.

Formulating an optimal Pricing mechanism is always dicey. Formulation based on IPP (Import Parity), EPP (Export Parity) or TPP (Trade parity) require a lot of deliberations considering oil companies diminishing GRMs as mentioned in the Parikh committee.

I will not go into the details which pricing mechanism is better, but to take a holistic view only to help discover any innovative idea.

Flexibility in Parity Pricing

Although international prices are out of control of the Government, it is the Government prerogative how the pricing formulae will be formulated. The automatic pricing formula which passes both benefit and burden to consumers is an option in relation to the changes in International pricing. This mechanism is being followed but to what extent is not known. As passing the entire burden on consumers will again attract criticism whereas passing the entire benefits will further alter the GRMs of refineries towards the lower side. Nonetheless, it is a good idea and practice to follow with restraint which will help both consumers and refiners to maximize their benefits. Here the challenge is that are we in a position to fix or monitor the prices on daily basis or weekly basis for passing the incremental benefits.

Instead of having one mechanism, we can have flexibility (is the key) in fixing prices by using all the parity models in combination from time to time which will optimize the under recoveries, addresses consumer concerns towards inflation, help bleeding oil companies to recover from cash crunch.

Hedging of prices

Government can also think for hedging of parity prices for corporates or bulk users based on some formulae or risk sharing mechanism. It will also address the issue of under recoveries. We can also have similar kind of mechanism for dealer margins.

Improving falling Rupee

Government can also look into the aspect of getting Rupee appreciation as the parity rates and crude purchase rates are in Dollars. If we take confidence building measures for the revival of economy, dollar will certainly take a little nose dive which will improve the pricing situation.

Reverse buying

We should also see importing of petroleum products by oil companies with zero duty applicability if the same is trading at lowest cost than fixed parity prices at any point in time.

Taxes and duties in Pricing (Controllable)

Is there any trade-off for reduction in taxes and duties?

It would not be anybody's case that petrol is cheap in India. It is a commodity consumed by both poor and rich. The petroleum sector represents a heady mix of opportunities and choices with great consequences on our lives, public finances and the environment. Taxes are only a part of the challenges facing consumers, enterprises and the government in dealing with this sector that drives our economy. The petroleum sector is a significant contributor to the tax revenue of the Centre and state governments.

The ultimate objective must be to strike a balance between the interests of the government for maximal revenues, the consumers for affordable prices and the companies for reasonable returns and a level playing field. This balance cannot be struck by merely focusing on the instrument of tax. The alignment of prices to the market has to be a key part of the recipe.

"It is interesting that we wake up to the tax rate on petroleum when there is a price shock. Any tax cut should be viewed in the context of its impact on the fiscal position"

Different states have different tax structure. A more optimal policy would be to reduce the central taxes and levy them on specific rather than on an ad valorem basis and bring petroleum within the ambit of the goods and services tax (GST). Such a policy would reduce the base of the sales tax or VAT and thereby, give oil companies the double benefit of reduced central and state taxes, bring predictability to the companies' tax liability and simplify the current complex and cumbersome tax structure. GST would streamline this to one rate.

Levying higher taxes was also justified on grounds

of encouraging energy conservation and the need for incentives to go for alternative sources of energy. Now, the consumer pays a hefty tax when it buys petrol, diesel or gas. Estimates attribute 50 per cent of the price of petroleum fuels to various taxes whether it is excise, customs or value-added tax (VAT) or sales. Indian consumer pays more for petrol compared to many other developing and developed countries. Both the Centre and states levy taxes on the petroleum sector. But increasingly, the sector has attracted attention not only for its taxes but also subsidies, reflecting the tangle of taxes and subsidies in which we are caught up in terms of collecting revenues, subsidising consumers and encouraging investment in the sector. Even the proposed goods and services tax leaves the petroleum sector out of its ambit.

When international crude prices rise, domestic consumers are partially insulated from the price shock in the short term, through subsidies and essentially taxes on upstream companies. The government also effectively borrows to meet the under-recoveries of oil marketing companies so that the consumer does not have to pay a higher price. If the question is only one: from which pocket do we pay the higher price – through borrowing, taxing upstream companies or through general fiscal resources – it probably would not have mattered. But would this be the best use of available resources? Should upstream companies use their resources for new investments to find fuel for the future? Which expenditures would the government have to reduce to meet the additional subsidy bill? Should cheaper diesel benefit the use of luxury automobiles? There are many questions that the taxes and subsidies in the petroleum sector raise when there is a global price shock. Of course, the exchange rate shock may have an added effect.

Clearly, this issue is embedded in a larger question that has an impact on an already delicate fiscal position. The question of reducing taxes on petroleum products cannot be addressed in isolation from the other factors that we have noted. It is also interesting that we wake up to the tax rate on petroleum when there is a price shock through higher crude oil prices. In other words, some sort of equilibrium is accepted before the new round of increase in prices. Any tax cut in the sector should be viewed in the context of its impact on the fiscal position: how will the government meet the revenue shortfall? Obviously, it cannot touch subsidies in the sector at the same time it reduces the taxes. This will not help the consumer. It may need to cut some other expenditure or run higher deficits. Without a more comprehensive approach to addressing at least the fiscal implications, merely cutting taxes on petrol would not lead to any real benefits. It has been mentioned that under-recoveries are recovered from the taxes.

In view of above explanations, the following recommendations may require deliberations:

1. A common tax structure across the state (GST) on rationale basis will not only give the level playing field for consumers across the states but also improves the faster cash flow to the Oil Companies.

2. As 35-40% constitutes the taxes in pricing, the same may be reviewed as how to strike balance between revenue generations and relaxing burden on consumers. We have to see or find out strike rate of conversion of revenue collected in terms of real development happening which in turn will increase the People Purchasing Power so that they can fight inflation. If we are doing that and bit of tweaking in the tax structure on lower side, will lessen the burden on common man.

3. Taxing the rich more and giving relaxtion to poor approach strategy when the prices goes out of the

roof to share burden and till prices come down to manageable levels, on the pretext that poor or common man are always hand to mouth and rich can shell out more money. This, however, require debate or some sort of mechanism to operate.

4. Since demand is inelastic for petroleum products, the revenue generations by way of taxes is the easy way out for Government to reduce the fiscal deficits. But if the Government can work out some strategies to curtail expenditures and seek other revenue generation models like getting better prices for spectrum, gas, oil and coal field auctions, we can definitely pass such benefits to consumers.

5. As most of the developed countries are not upgrading their refining capacities, whereas Indian Refiners continue to consolidate their capacities by way of Greenfield Refinery and upgrading their existing capacities, India may become an export hub in the near future after meeting the indigenous demand, Government can look to encash the opportunities in a big way to get their coffers filled with revenues.

6. Opening of more COCO to take care of dealer margins.

Parting message

"Take away of the Book : The story of Geese flight."

India has to take fresh guard and require fresh legs and creative minds of youngsters to rewrite history. The success of talented middle class heading various high profile posts of many prestigious companies worldwide is very reassuring (only silver lining in the dark cloud). We require a captain who can steady the ship, have vision and mission, takes tough decisions and hit fours and sixes every now and then, to make India a force to reckon with, on the horizon of the world, at least when India becomes 80 years old. We should start afresh forgetting all the negativities (Like *ab kuch nahi ho sakta*- Nothing can be done now). The positive thing is that we have progressed considerably after independence but the degree of progress requires to be done at a faster pace now.

Please remember one of the famous Gita recitals in Sanskrit made by Lord Krishna:-

यदा यदा ही धर्मस्य ग्लानिभर्वति भारत,
अभ्युथानम् अधर्मस्य तदात्मानं सृजाम्यहम्।
परित्राणाय साधुनाम विनाशाय चः दुष्कृताम,
धर्म संस्थापनार्थाय सभ्भावामी युगे युगे।।

Translation

Whenever there is decline of Dharma (righteousness)...And rise of Adharma (unrighteousness);

To protect the virtuous. To destroy the wicked and to re-establish Dharma, I manifest myself, through the ages.

The situation today in India is such that even Lord Krishna will require manifestation several times to change the mindset of the people. We have to do *atm-manthan* (Self-digging) and also by way of collective wisdom to get the real *Amrit* (Holy Liquid which came out during Amrit Manthan done by *Devta* and *Asur*) of Success and get the *Vish* (Poison) of hatred out with focus on India winning always.

For India's success, before signing–off, I will just recite few lines of old Hindi song which has been inspirational during India rebuilding days after independence:

"Chodo kal ki bateein, kal ki baat purani, Naye Dur mein likhengey mil kar naiye kahani- Hum Hindustani"

It means, we Indians should forget our past (whatever has happened has happened), will have to work harder to change the skyline, flooded with success stories of India Winning and India Shining in real or measured terms. Remember, we should work for the success of our operation/project "Bharat Vijai Bhavo". Let us join hand folks and it is now or never as famously coined by the then Indian Captain Saurav Ganguly during 2003 Cricket World Cup.

The crux or the take-away of the book is highlighted in the story of geese flight. I thank the author of the story with great regard of bringing such a story to make people understand how team work can do wonders. I am just reproducing the same once again before saying a FINAL GOODBYE.

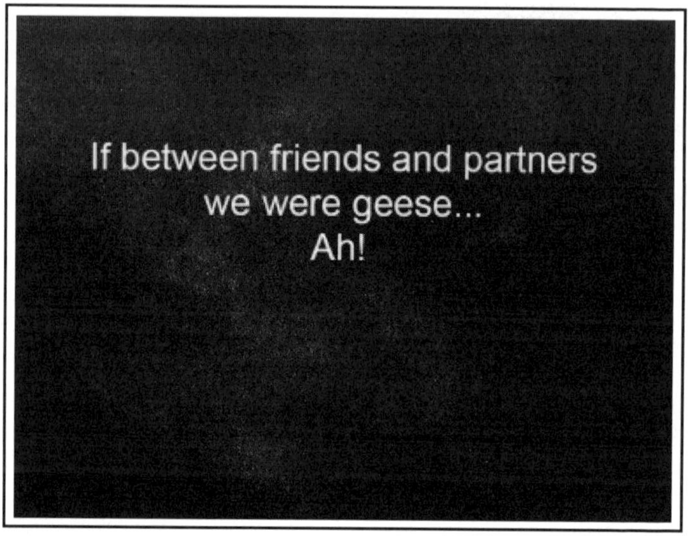
If between friends and partners
we were geese...
Ah!

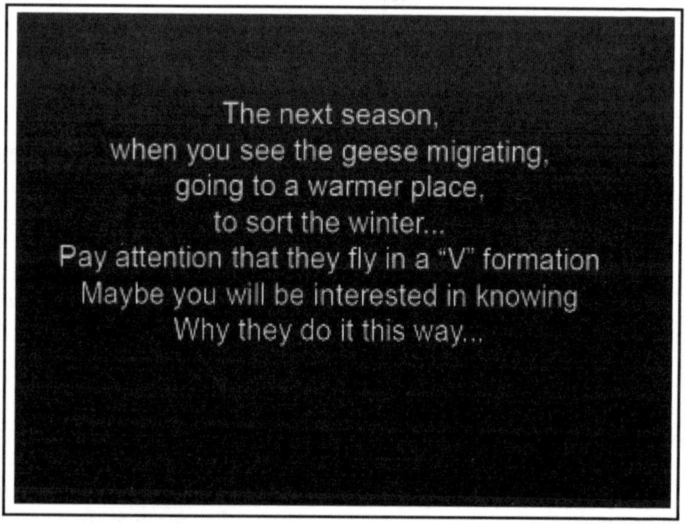
The next season,
when you see the geese migrating,
going to a warmer place,
to sort the winter...
Pay attention that they fly in a "V" formation
Maybe you will be interested in knowing
Why they do it this way...

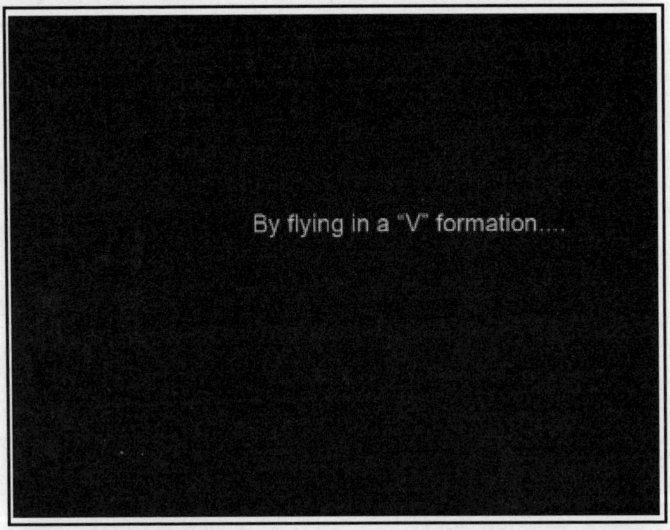
By flying in a "V" formation....

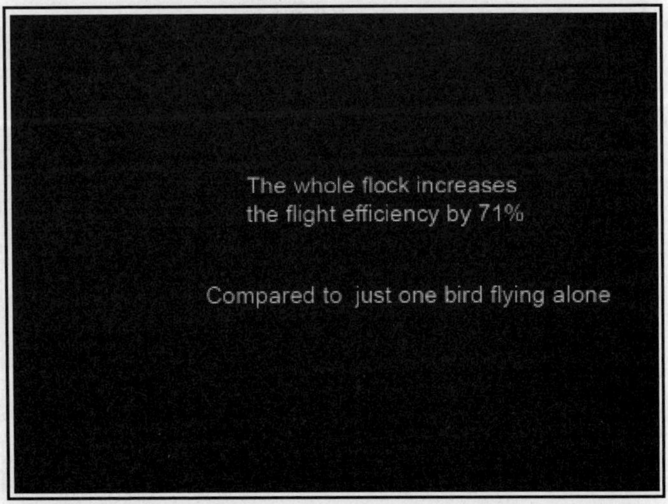
The whole flock increases
the flight efficiency by 71%
Compared to just one bird flying alone

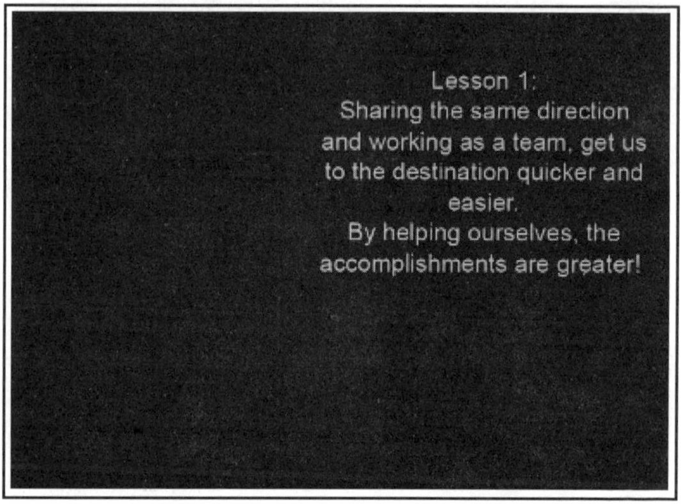
Lesson 1:
Sharing the same direction and working as a team, get us to the destination quicker and easier.
By helping ourselves, the accomplishments are greater!

When a goose leaves the formation

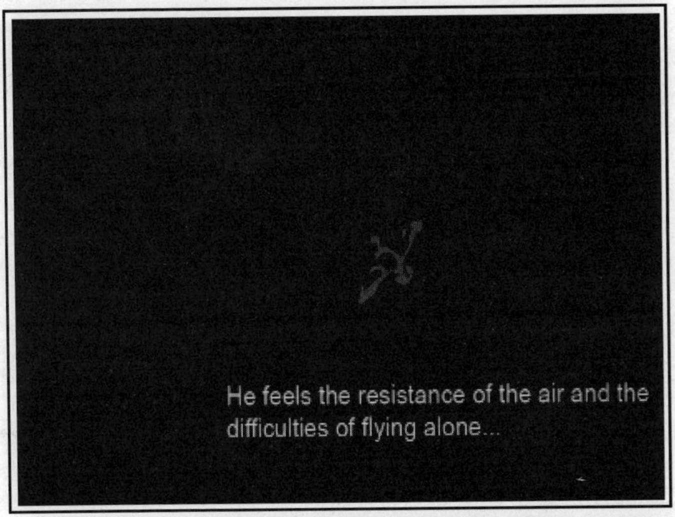
He feels the resistance of the air and the
difficulties of flying alone...

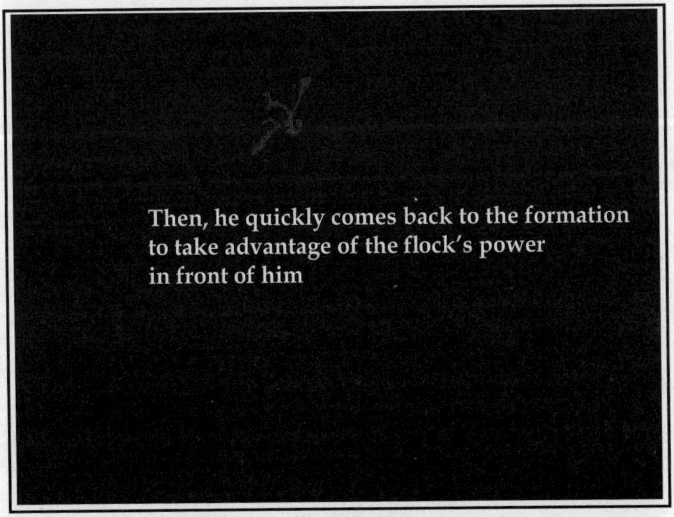
Then, he quickly comes back to the formation
to take advantage of the flock's power
in front of him

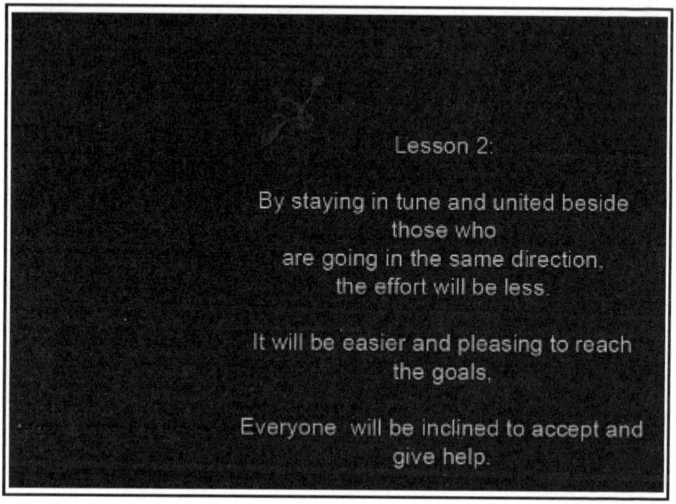
Lesson 2:
By staying in tune and united beside those who
are going in the same direction,
the effort will be less.
It will be easier and pleasing to reach the goals,
Everyone will be inclined to accept and give help.

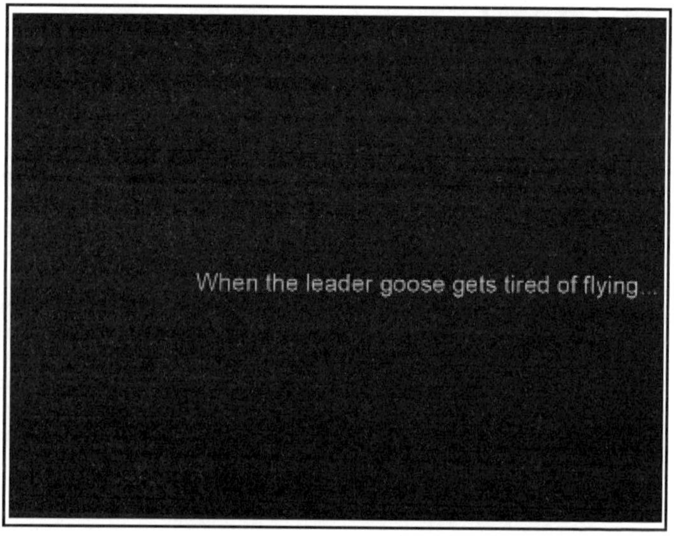
When the leader goose gets tired of flying...

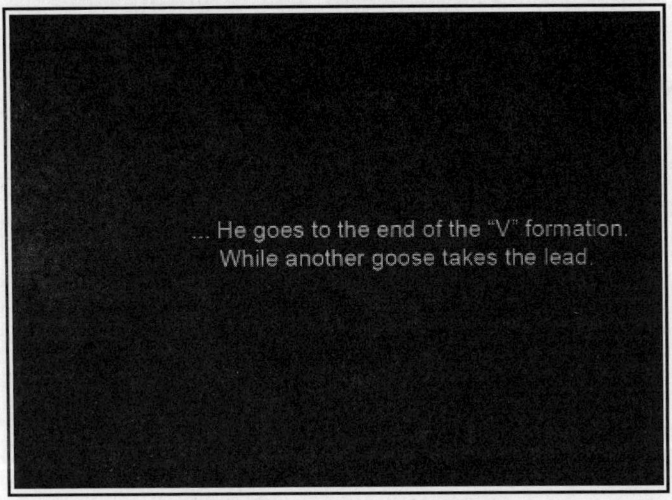
... He goes to the end of the "V" formation.
While another goose takes the lead.

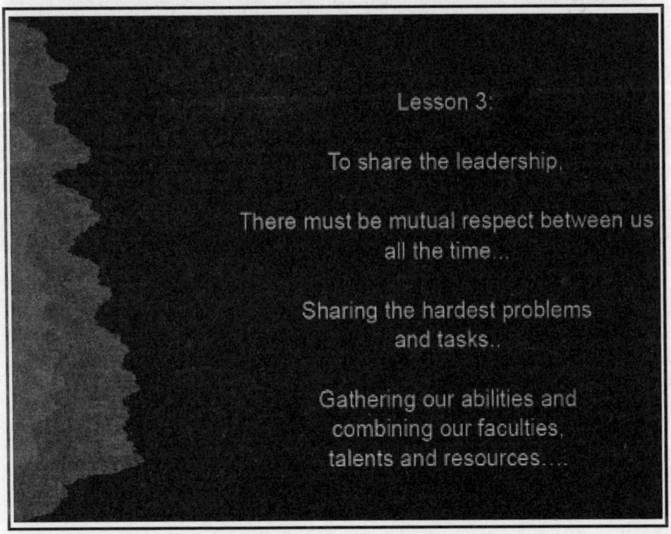
Lesson 3:
To share the leadership,
There must be mutual respect between us all the time...
Sharing the hardest problems and tasks..
Gathering our abilities and combining our faculties, talents and resources....

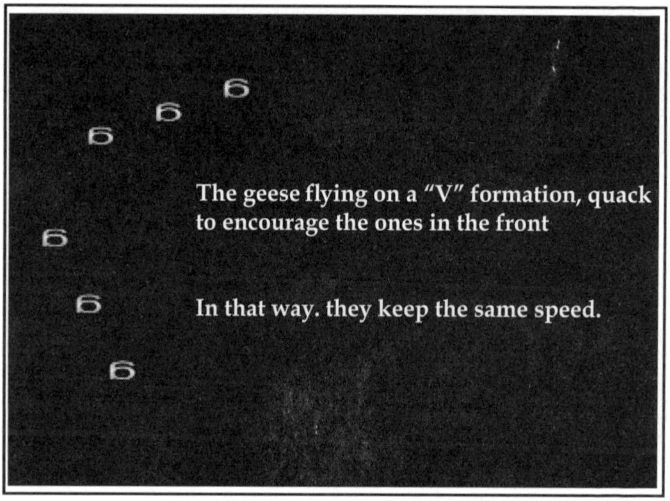
The geese flying on a "V" formation, quack to encourage the ones in the front
In that way. they keep the same speed.

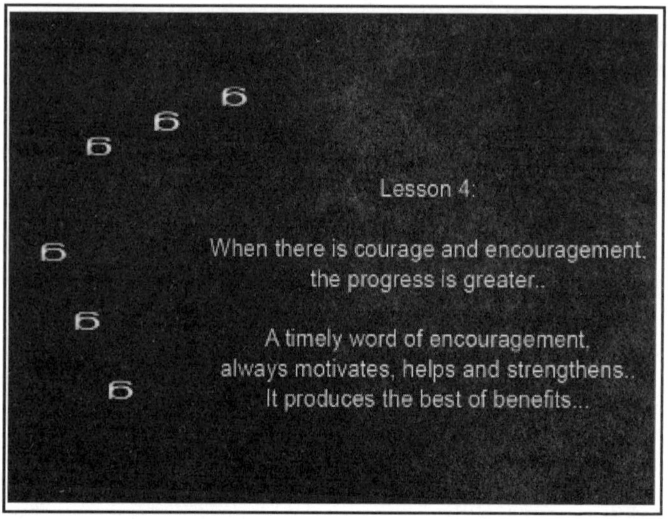
Lesson 4:
When there is courage and encouragement, the progress is greater..
A timely word of encouragement, always motivates, helps and strengthens.. It produces the best of benefits...

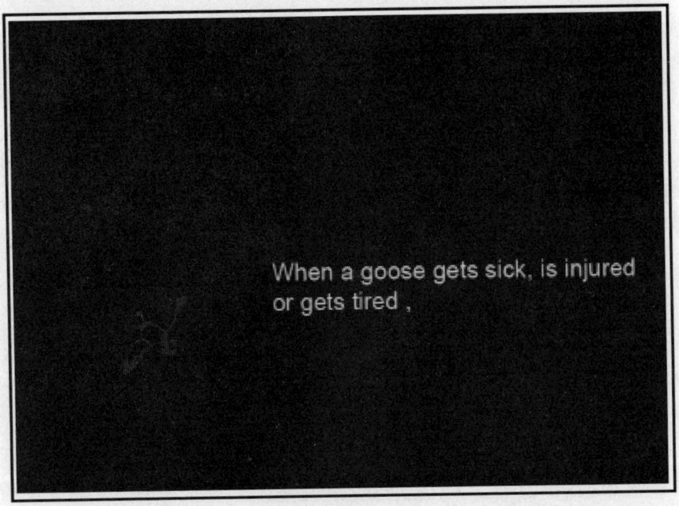
When a goose gets sick, is injured
or gets tired ,

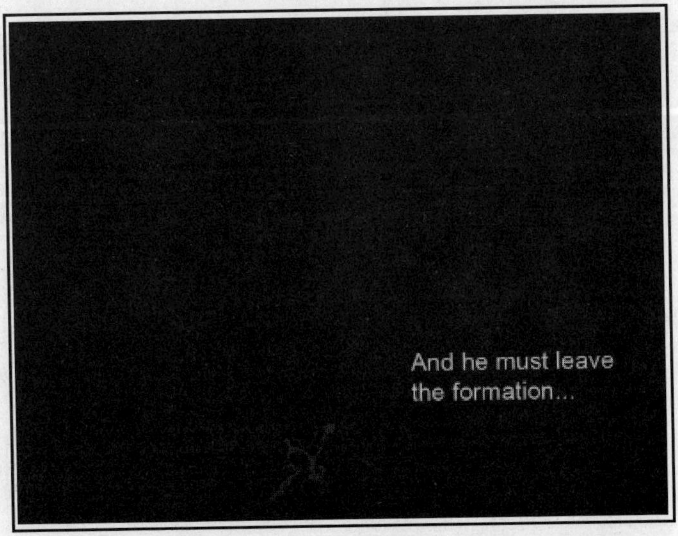
And he must leave
the formation...

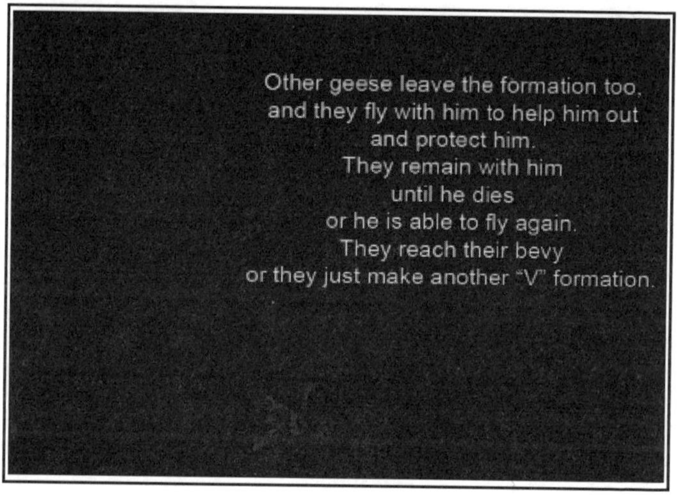
Other geese leave the formation too,
and they fly with him to help him out
and protect him.
They remain with him
until he dies
or he is able to fly again.
They reach their bevy
or they just make another "V" formation.

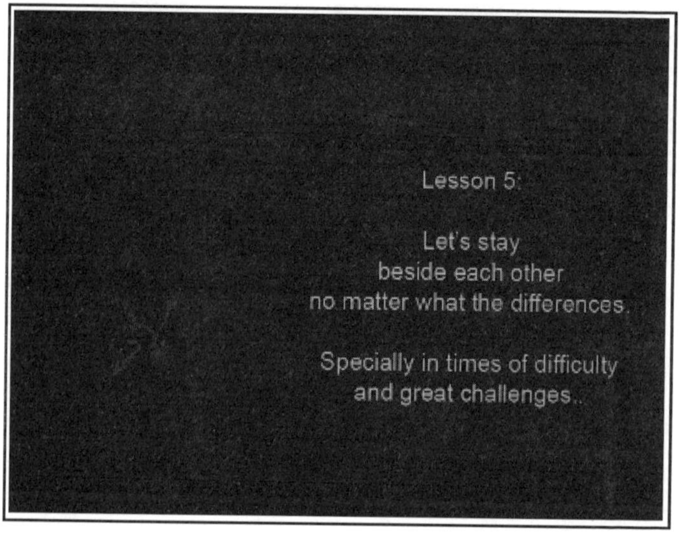
Lesson 5:
Let's stay
beside each other
no matter what the differences.
Specially in times of difficulty
and great challenges..

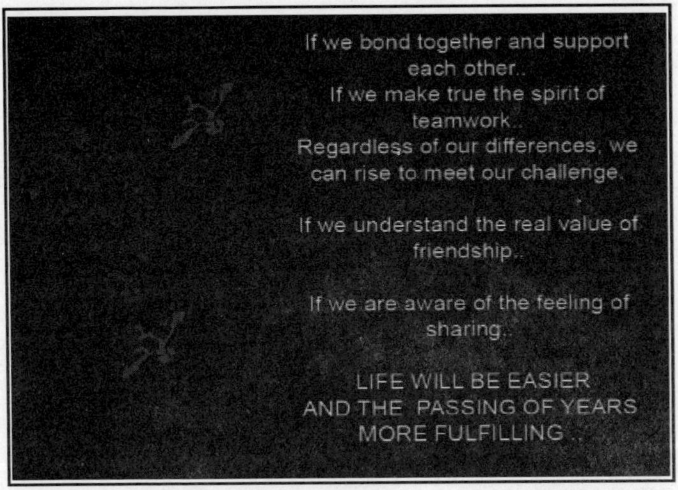
If we bond together and support each other..
If we make true the spirit of teamwork..
Regardless of our differences, we can rise to meet our challenge.
If we understand the real value of friendship..
If we are aware of the feeling of sharing..
LIFE WILL BE EASIER
AND THE PASSING OF YEARS
MORE FULFILLING ..

MY FRIENDS AND PARTNERS...
LET'S BE LIKE THE GEESE!!!

Part-5

Frequently Asked Questions(FAQs)

"Keep Things Simple"

Q.1 What is the USP of this book?

Ans *Its simplicity and the ideas floated in the book coupled* *with real life examples, people can relate themselves easily. This will make everybody count and will make them feel important. This book is like homecoming.*

Q.2 Is winning unidirectional?

Ans *To have Winning count and to sustain it, it should be multidirectional. You may get pole position in life but its sustenance depends how much Human Touch theory you practiced to get applause from bête-noire as well.*

Q.3 Why only few people sustain success?

Ans *They have lessons learnt of earlier decisions in their mind as archives and refer to them before taking future decisions wherever required.*

Q.4 Why some people fade away after achieving super success?

Ans *I know everything and will do no wrong results in their failure.*

Q.5 Why are we short of time?

Ans *Time is the essence of everything. Time is money, Time to market and Time lost is opportunity lost is the jargons used today. We see things as we are made to see. We never apply our minds or reorganize ourselves.*

Q.6 Can time be timed?

Ans *Yes, if you keep your bosses, peers, subordinates and most importantly your wife happy.*

Q.7 What if everything went haywire?

Ans *Wait for the time to change or else change the time. The former is more conducive. Arvind Kejriwal (Ex-Chief Minister of Delhi) was the victim of opening too many fronts and not able to reconcile.*

Q.8 Why everybody is trying so hard and are stressed out?

Ans *People are not able to keep things simple. They provide solutions which are more dangerous than the problem itself.*

Q.9 Being a leader or a good team member will do?

Ans *A leader is a good team member as well. So, if you prove your mantle as a good team member you automatically will be chosen as natural leader for the next assignment.*

Q.10 Is the Boss always right?

Ans *The Boss is always dependent on your inputs. So provide them with the right inputs so that he will ALWAYS find difficult to counter.*

Q.11 China vs India- Who is economically a more viable country ?

Ans *The answer is China at Present but we have the intellectual property in terms of talented young middle class duly recognized by the world to turn it around in the next 10-20 years as evident from the appointment of Shri Satya Nadella as Microsoft chief.*

Q.12 Why are we still lagging?

Ans *We are on the pull side of the door. We pull everything down and do not push or use collective wisdom.*

Q.13 What if India fails to deliver?

Ans *China will laugh all the way and will continue to have free run.*

Q.14 Who will deliver Top leadership or people down the lane ?

Ans *As it is rightly said that the bottom line does not only mean profit, it is the wealth created for the people will do wonder. Initially, Top-Down and finally Bottoms up approach will help us to enjoy economies of scale.*

Q.15 Who is the real winner of Lok Sabha Elections 2014?

Ans *People of India are the real winners of the best ever elections.*

Q.16 What made our new Prime Minister Shri Narendra Modi (NaMo as referred in the media), click in the election?

Ans *His single minded approach to make "Bharat Vijai Bhavo".*

Q.17 Will the present New Government deliver?

Ans *It is a million dollar question as of now. However a proven leader at the Top with decisive mandate – the best ever possible scenario will at least calm down the nerves of millions of Indians to say that "**Achey Din Anney Wale Hain.**"*

Q.18 What does the common man require immediately?

Ans *Taming Inflation. Restructuring the tax structure is the key to have prices of essential commodities especially petroleum product prices down.*

Q.19 Will India ever regain its Golden Era?

Ans *Yes, If we all become change managers towards common objective to make "Bharat Vijai Bhavo".*

Q.20 How to die peacefully knowing that you are successful?

Ans *Be a good Human Being, a good effective team member and a finisher.*

Index